24.9.02

To

Billu and Swayam

On Your Silver Wedding Anniversary

With Love -

Sae Ca -

D1112483

The Women's Jokebook

The Women's Jokebook

The horrible truth about what men are really like!

by Marcie Starr

To [illegible]

With Love –

[illegible]

First published in Great Britain by
Arcturus Publishing Limited
First Floor
1-7 Shand Street
London
SE1 2ES

for Index Books
Henson Way
Kettering
Northants
NN16 8PX

This edition published 2000

Printed and bound in Finland

Text Design by Zeta @ Moo

ISBN 1 84193 043 1

CONTENTS

FOREWORD......7

MEN AT BRAGGING......9

MEN AT BALANCING THE BOOKS......21

MEN AT DEATH'S DOOR......29

MEN AT FATHERHOOD......37

MEN AT LOVE......47

MEN AT MEDICINE......65

MEN AT MARRIAGE......75

MEN AT PLAY......91

MEN AT SENILITY......99

MEN AT SIMPLE-MINDEDNESS......107

MEN AT SPORT......125

MEN AT THE BAR......129

MEN AT THE BUTT END......137

MEN AT THEIR WEAKEST......153

MEN AT THEIR WORST......167

MEN AT TRAVEL......179

MEN AT WORK......185

FOREWORD

What have you got when you have two little balls in your hand?
A man's undivided attention.

Here we have men "being men". A humorous, irrelevant look at the male species, the human cockbird as he struts his stuff, flashes his feathers and then... falls flat on his face.

You'll find men as boys - and are they ever anything else - to man as the hopeless liar, the hapless lover, the helpless father.

You'll recognise the "ill man" where only he can make a drama into a crisis. The flash man who's bulb always bursts at the crucial moment. The sportsman who still thinks he has a six pack when in fact he wears a beer belly.

For men, this book acts as a mirror that doesn't lie and for women, the ultimate hilarious recognition of what we have always known - when he says it is six and a half, it is actually only four!

What's the difference between pink and purple?
The woman's grip.

Enjoy!

MEN AT BRAGGING

I wouldn't say he was handsome - but he would.

* * *

Whoever said all men are created equal never went to a nudist colony.

* * *

"Now just think about it, Doreen, how on earth can you take men seriously when they've got willies?"

* * *

Did you hear about the vain man who shaved his pubic hair once every two days?
He thought designer stubble was "hip" all over.

* * *

A very bitter wife went with her husband to buy him some new trousers. After he had been measured up for them, the tailor asked him if he preferred buttons or a zip.
"A zip, please," replied the man.
"And would sir like a 5" or 10" zip?"
"Ten," he replied.
Moments later they left the shop and the wife looked at him furiously.
"You and your 10" zip! You remind me of our next door neighbour. He's the only man in the street to have a double garage, yet every morning when he opens the huge doors, he wheels his bicycle out."

A pompous university lecturer demanded total attention from his students when he was lecturing. However, in his Tuesday morning class, one girl would sit there and knit continuously throughout the lesson. After a month of this, he couldn't stand it any longer and spoke angrily to her.
"Are you aware that some 19th century psychiatrists believed knitting was a form of masturbation?"
She replied smoothly, "Is that so, professor? Then you do it your way and I'll do it mine."

* * *

Men are vainer than women though they don't use make-up - they think they don't need it.

* * *

A man was caught short and had to rush behind some fencing to have a pee. Unknown to him, a mother and her daughter were looking out of their bedroom window and had a perfect view of his activities. Suddenly he heard laughter and looking up, saw the daughter in hysterics.
"Hey!" he shouted, "can't you keep your daughter in order, it's very rude of her."
The mother replied "Oh don't mind her, she's still young and she laughs at any little thing."

* * *

How many men does it take to screw in a light bulb?
Six. One to screw it in and the other five to brag about how he screwed it.

* * *

Two women were discussing their sexual experiences. The first said she'd been living in the east, where men's tackle tended to be long and thin.
"Well, that's odd," replied her friend, "because I've been in the west, where they're usually short and thick."
A little later, one of the daughters who had overheard the earlier conversation told her mother she hoped to marry someone from the foreign office. Puzzled, her mother asked why.
"Well, with any luck, he'll have been born in the west but spent a lot of his working life in the east."

* * *

What did the fat woman say to the fat man?
Thanks for the tip.

* * *

Cocky Rocky was well known in the village for his obsession with body building. Every morning he would go down to the local gym, change into his lycra costume and spend the morning making out on the weights. He never spoke to anyone, he'd just grin stupidly as he listened to his Walkman. Month after month this went on. Rocky would never mix with the others, he'd just grin stupidly at himself in the mirror, rubbing himself down with oil and listening to the Walkman, which he was always carrying.
"Bloody stuck-up sod," muttered one of the regular gym goers, "I'll cut him down to size."
He walked over to where Rocky was standing. "Hey, you! too good for us, are you?"
But Rocky didn't hear him, he was listening to his Walkman.
"Hey, you!" repeated the man, pulling the Walkman off Rocky's head but in doing so, Rocky fell to the ground and died almost immediately.
As they took the body away, the shocked man picked up the

Walkman and put it to his ear. All he heard was 'Breathe in...breathe out...breathe in...'

* * *

A man is never surprised when a woman admires him, but is always surprised when she admires another man.

* * *

What did the girl say to the arrogant man?
Is it in?

* * *

What does a man with a 12" dick have for breakfast?
Well, this morning I had cornflakes, followed by...

* * *

A man was walking home from the pub when he discovered an old magic lamp lying in a skip. As he rubbed it, a genie appeared and gave him the chance to have one wish. Rather embarrassed, the man said he was unhappy over the size of his private parts. Could he have a bigger one, please?
So the wish was granted and the man continued walking home. But by the time he got to the bottom of his street, his dick had grown past his knees and was still travelling. Quick as a flash, he stumbled back to the skip and spoke to the genie again.
"I'm sorry to sound ungrateful," he said, "but may I have just one more wish?"
"And what's that?"asked the genie.
"May I have longer legs?"

* * *

"Mrs Jones, you are up before the court for assaulting your husband, resulting in hospitalisation. How do you plead?"
"Guilty, Your Honour," said the timid little wife.
The judge looked surprised at this poor wretched woman and asked her kindly:
"Well, tell us in your own words, what happened?"
She began, "I'd locked Arthur out of the bedroom because he'd come home staggering and smelling strongly of booze. But later on he started hammering on the door. At first I ignored him, but then he said I'd be sure to let him in if I knew what he was knocking with." The woman dabbed her eyes and continued. "So, of course, Your Honour, I jumped up to let him in and he was standing there (sob) with a box of chocolates in his hand!"

* * *

"My husband doesn't have a lot to say. Sadly you have to listen for quite some time to find that out."

* * *

An arrogant young man drove his girlfriend home after their first date and pulled up outside her home. After a few good night kisses, he got his penis out and put it in her hand.
"How dare you!" she exclaimed and immediately got out of the car and walked up the garden path. As she arrived at the door, she turned and shouted, "I've only got two words to say to you, GET LOST."
"And I've got two for you," he yelled. "LET GO."

* * *

"Julie," said the boastful man, "will you rate my performance on a scale of one to ten?"
"Of course, darling...May I use fractions?"

A group of men were standing at the bar talking, when one of them boasted he could pull the bird at the table in front of them. With an arrogant swagger, he walked up to her and said, "Hey, beautiful, haven't I seen you somewhere before?"
"Yes," she said loudly, "I work at the VD clinic."

* * *

A young woman became an avid gardener. Her flowers were the best for miles around and her vegetables flourished. However, amongst all this there was one disappointment. She could not get her tomatoes to ripen. One day, as she was gloomily looking at them, her neighbour peered over the fence and asked her what was wrong.
"It's my tomatoes," she wailed, "they won't go red."
"No problem," he replied. "Do as I do to my tomatoes. Each evening I expose myself to them and they turn red with embarrassment."
So every evening in the following week, the woman stripped naked and exposed herself to her tomatoes. The next time she met her neighbour, he asked how things were going.
"No luck with the tomatoes," she replied, "but you should see the size of my carrots!"

* * *

Three nuns were discussing their recent holidays. The first was describing, with her hands, the huge melons she'd seen in Miami. The second nun nodded in approval and then described, with her hands, the massive bananas she'd seen in Jamaica.
The third, who was deaf, then asked, "Father who?"

* * *

Two women talking over the garden wall.
"Do you know, Trace, I knew I'd married Mr Right. I just didn't realise his first name was Always!"

Did you hear about the man who was so vain, every time there was lightning, he thought someone was taking his picture.

* * *

The couple had been courting for more than six months and the man decided to become more amorous. He unzipped his trousers and put his willy in the girl's hand.
"This is for you," he said boastfully.
"Oh, no thanks," she replied. "You know I don't smoke."

* * *

"Ha, ha!" laughed the man mischievously, "I wonder what people would say if they could see me lying here on this beach absolutely starkers."
"They'd say I married you for your money," replied his wife.

* * *

Why do women have trouble parking the car?
Because they're always being told that 4" is 8".

* * *

An over-protective father decided to test his three daughters' innocence by discovering how much they know about sex. He called his first daughter into the room, dropped his trousers, pointed to his manhood and said, "Do you know what this is?"
"Of course, father," replied the daughter, "that's your penis."
"What!" exclaimed the shocked father, "How dare you use such words? Leave this house immediately."
Then he called in his second daughter, "Do you know what this is?" he said, pointing once again at his todger.
"Yes, father," she replied, "that's your willy".
"Get out of here!" he shouted, "I don't want to hear such filth."

Then his youngest daughter came in and was asked the same question."
"I really don't know," she replied.
"Oh my beautiful innocent daughter," he said smiling, "that, my darling, is a penis."
"What!" she exclaimed, "you call that a penis!"

* * *

A very vain man is determined to get an all-over tan which he has almost achieved apart from his todger. So he takes himself off to a deserted part of the beach and buries himself in the sand, just leaving his willy sticking up to get the sun's rays. A short time passes when, from out of the blue, two old ladies appear and notice this strange phenomenon.
"Look at that, Flo, it's just not damned fair," says the first woman.
"How come, Sal?" asks Flo.
"When I was 7, I was glad I didn't have one. When I was 17, I wanted to know more about it. When I was 27 I loved it. When I was 47, I went looking for it. When I was 67 I had a hard time getting it and when I was 77, I gave up. But now, here we are, I'm 87, and the bloody things are growing wild."

* * *

A man picks up a girl in a singles bar. They go out to dinner, then return to his flat, where they soon end up in bed. Afterwards he turns to her and says:
"Am I the first man you've ever been to bed with?"
She looks at him for a moment or two and replies,
"You might be, your face looks familiar."

* * *

What has a thousand teeth and holds back a monster?
"My fly zip," said the arrogant man.

"Do you think I'm vain and boastful?" the man asked his girlfriend.
"Not too bad," she replied. "Why do you ask?"
"Because most men as handsome as me usually are."

* * *

The man looked into his bedroom mirror and proudly observed his naked body. "Do you know, Doreen, just two more inches and I'd be a king."
His wife retorted quickly, "Just three inches less and you'd be a queen."

* * *

Who is the most popular man at the nudist colony?
The guy who can carry two coffees and ten doughnuts.

* * *

How can a weak wally make his girlfriend laugh?
By getting his pecker out.

* * *

There was a very vain man who was never satisfied with the way he looked. One day he found a magic mirror in an old junk shop and getting it home, he stood before it and chanted:
"Mirror, mirror on the wall, make my manhood touch the floor."
Suddenly there was an almighty whoosh, and the man's legs fell off.

* * *

It is probably true to say that when a group of men get together, and they've all had a few beers, they will start to brag.
One Tuesday lunchtime in a quiet bar on the side of the A34, four

men were boasting about the size of their todgers. After a heated argument, they eventually decided to get them out and measure them. So, in a flash, all four were lying out on the top of the bar when in walked a gay bloke.
"Oh my!" he exclaimed. "Buffet."

* * *

Maurice was 48 and very vain. He spent hours in front of the mirror, using anti-wrinkle cream and exercising with weights. He prided himself that most people would think he was younger than his age.
One morning, to boost his ego, he asked the woman in the post office how old she thought he was.
"Oh, I would guess you were 39," she said.
The man was gratified to see the look on her face when he told her he was actually 48. Sometime later he sat down next to an old spinster in the park and he couldn't help but ask the woman how old she thought he was.
"Well, young man," she said, "I can't see so well but if I had a feel of your willy, I'm sure I could give you the correct answer."
Somewhat startled but curious, the man agreed. He unzipped his trousers and the old woman had a right good fondle.
"Oh, yes," she confirmed, "you're 48."
"That's amazing!" he gasped. "How did you know that?"
The old woman blushed and replied, "Actually I was standing behind you in the post office."

* * *

An arrogant young man, with an awful line in chat-up patter, told his girlfriend he was going to screw her like she'd never been screwed before. Later that night in bed, once the business had been done, she took a feather and started hitting him on the head with it.
"What are you doing?" he asked.
"Well, comparatively speaking, I suppose I'm beating your brains out."

Colin was always bragging about his body. One day he had a picture taken of himself in the nude and he gave it to his girlfriend.
"What do you think of that then?" he asked proudly.
"Mmmm," she replied, "I think I'll get it enlarged."

* * *

A woman spotted a hulking great man on the dance floor who had the biggest feet she had ever seen. Now, because she's heard that the bigger the man's feet, the larger his tackle, she set her eyes on him. Lo and behold, by the end of the night, she'd succeeded and they went back to his flat together.
However, the next morning she left very early, leaving a note pinned to the duvet.
"Here's £20. Next time buy a pair of shoes that fit you properly."

* * *

He turned to his wife and said, "Whenever I pass a mirror, I have to stop and look at myself just to make sure I'm as perfect as ever. Do you think I'm vain?"
"No, darling, just very imaginative."

* * *

"Kiss me, sweetheart, and I'll tell you a secret," said the cocky young man.
She retorted, "I know your secret. I work at the clinic."

* * *

A vain, middle-aged man suffers a heart attack and is rushed to hospital. While they are working on him, he has a near-death experience. God speaks to him saying that it is too soon for him to join them. He still has thirty years to live.

The man makes a complete recovery and decides he is going to enjoy life to the full.
Top of the agenda is to make himself even more irresistible to women. He gets his nose changed, has his teeth capped, dyes his hair and has a face lift. Then he starts going down the gym twice a week to pump some iron.
Two months later he's a different man. Feeling really great about himself, he decides to take a walk through the park, but as he crosses the road a truck careers towards him out of control and kills him stone dead. When he gets to heaven, he says to God angrily, "Hey! You told me I had another thirty years to live."
"Well, I'm sorry," says God, "I just didn't recognise you."

* * *

Here are three words guaranteed to destroy a man's ego.
"Is it in?"

* * *

The arrogant unattractive man went to the photographer's and demanded, "Make sure your photos do me justice."
"Sir," he replied haughtily, "you don't want justice, you want mercy."

* * *

"Hi, the name's Thomas, John Thomas."
"Well, I'm Holly, so I'm used to little pricks."

* * *

MEN AT BALANCING THE BOOKS

Why do bankers make the best lovers?
They know the penalties for an early withdrawal.

* * *

Said the bitter woman to her friend, "When the only thing that's stiff is his socks, then it's time to take the money and run."

* * *

A husband and wife were having a flaming argument about their money problems.
"If it wasn't for my money, that Porsche and that swimming pool wouldn't be here."
She retorted, "If it wasn't for your money, I wouldn't be here!"

* * *

"Hello Josie, you look preoccupied this morning," remarked her friend.
"I am a bit," she replied. "This morning my boyfriend lost all his money on the stock market."
"How awful! You must feel so sorry for him."
"I am. I'm just wondering how he will cope without me."

* * *

A bloke walked into a butcher's shop and picked up a chicken. He examined it closely, sniffing under the wings and looking up the rear

end. After a couple of minutes he turned to the man behind the counter and said accusingly, "This chicken's not fresh."
"Excuse me, sir," replied the offended butcher, "could you pass the same test?"

* * *

A man was set upon by muggers as he walked down the dark street. Although there were four of them, the victim put up a good fight but was eventually battered to the ground with broken ribs and a broken nose.
One of the muggers went through his pockets and to his amazement found 54p.
"Hey, why did you put up such a fight for a measly 54p?" asked the mugger.
The poor man gasped in pain, "I didn't know that's all you were after," he moaned. "I thought it was the £200 I had in my shoe."

* * *

Every wife likes her husband to have something tender about him, especially legal tender.

* * *

A man buys a packet of salted nuts and gives one to his wife. Five minutes later she asks for another one.
"Why do you want another one?" he replies. "They all taste the same."

* * *

A rich young man was involved in a very bad car crash, and his Porsche was a write-off. As he lay stunned at the side of the road, he moaned quietly to himself, "Oh, my car, my poor car".

A paramedic overheard his words and knelt down beside him.
"Excuse me, sir," he said gently, "I think you should be more concerned about your arm."
The young man looked down to where his arm should have been and started to cry in anguish, "Oh my Rolex, my Rolex!"

* * *

Lady Highbrow was sitting in her bedroom when her butler walked into the room. "Marlow, how many times do I have to tell you, don't walk into my room without knocking first. There could be times when it would be very embarrassing," she said.
"Nothing to worry about, ma'am," he replied. "I always check first by looking through the keyhole."

* * *

On another occasion, Lady Highbrow was forced to sack her cook.
"It's no good, Dorothy, you are unable to maintain the standards I expect. Your cooking is boring and the state of the kitchen is a disgrace."
"Well, good riddance to this flaming job," retorted the cook. "Not everyone in this house thinks I'm bad. Your husband says I do a great coq au vin and what's more, I'm better in bed than you are."
"What!" roared Lady Highbrow. "Who told you that? My husband?"
"No, the gardener, so there!!"

* * *

What's your idea of a perfect husband?
A man with a £1 million life insurance who dies on his wedding night.

* * *

A woman rushed into the lounge to find her husband asleep on the sofa. "Quick, Jack, get up. I've just won the £20 million jackpot. Get packing and ring the bus station."
Jack jumped up. "What shall I ask for? What's the destination?"
"I don't care," she replied, "just as long as you're out of here before lunch-time."

* * *

What do a man and the tax office have in common?
They're both impossible to get through to when you want to talk.

* * *

"George, I'm going shopping. Can I have some money?" asked the wife.
"Money, money, money, that's all you ever ask me for. Sometimes I think you need more brains than more money."
"Maybe, darling," she replied calmly, "but then again I thought I'd only ask you for what you had most of!"

* * *

Any girl can live on love - if he's wealthy.

* * *

A man was talking to his mate in the pub about his financial problems.
"It's no good Tony, I'm going to sit down with my wife tonight and tell her a few home truths. She has no idea about money."
The next day they met up again and Tony asked how it went.
"Oh great," he replied, "we've sorted things out. I'm going to give up beer and football."

* * *

A very insecure man was anxious to know how much his wife loved him.
"Darling, if I was horribly injured in a car crash and had to spend the rest of my days in a wheelchair, would you still love me?"
"Of course I would, sweetheart," she replied, "I'll always love you."
He continued, "And if I became impotent and could no longer make love to you, would you still love me?"
"Don't be silly, I'll always love you," she replied.
"And if I lost all my money on the stock market, would you still love me?"
She looked at him for a moment and then said, "Sweetheart, I've told you, I will always love you...and I'll miss you terribly."

* * *

On the eve of his marriage a man was having last-minute doubts.
"Oh Julie, you're not just marrying me because I've inherited £1 million from my late uncle?"
"Of course not," she replied, "I'd marry you no matter who left you the money."

* * *

Lady Challerton called for her manservant.
"Jeeves," she said, "take off my shoes, take off my coat, take off my dress, take off my stockings and take off my bra and lacy knickers. Now Jeeves, one more thing, I don't ever want to see you wearing them again."

* * *

A despicable young man heard that his elderly aunt only had six months to live. Now his aunt was very rich and doted on her two Siamese cats. So the young man decided to curry favour with his aunt, hoping that she would be generous to him in her will.

Every week he would travel to her house and make a big fuss of the cats, feeding them, grooming them and even taking them for walks. Six months went by and the old lady died. Sure enough she remembered him in her will. She left him her cats!

* * *

Two tight-fisted men, Graham and Robert, were on a mountaineering holiday in Scotland when Graham slipped badly and ended up hanging by his fingertips over a crevasse.
"Quick, Bob," he screamed, "get down to the village and buy a rope. I don't know how long I can hang on here."
Bob raced off, leaving Graham hanging there and after 20 minutes his grip was beginning to weaken. Then to his relief, he heard Bob returning.
"Hurry up, help me quick," he yelled, "have you got the rope?"
"No," said Bob, "those greedy buggers in the village wanted £10 for it."

* * *

A famous Hollywood star was standing naked at the bedroom window doing his exercises. Suddenly his wife came into the room, rushed over to the window and pulled the curtains.
"You idiot," she hissed, "if people see you, they'll think I only married you for your money."

* * *

Harry, the old skinflint, was sitting by his wife's bed. She was desperately ill and had very little time to live.
"Martha," whispered Harry, "I've got to get down to the post office to collect my pension. If you feel yourself going before I get back, will you turn the light off."

When do you care for a man's company?
When he owns it.

* * *

A young man was keen to buy his girlfriend a very special present but, unsure of what to get, he took her sister along to help him choose. A little later, they decided to buy her some gloves - something not too personal but at the same time something that she would wear often and think of him.
As he gave the gloves to the assistant to be wrapped, the sister had also been buying for herself and handed in a pair of knickers. However, unknown to the two buyers, the assistant muddled up the packages and they both got each other's purchase.
Sadly, the boyfriend didn't check his package before sending it off. He simply wrote the following note to go with it.

My darling,
I hope you like the enclosed gift. I bought them because I notice you never wear any when we go out together and your sister thought the short ones were better than the longer ones because they're easier to remove. I hope you like the colour. I know they're a little light but the lady in the shop showed me the ones she's been wearing for the past month and there was hardly a mark on them. She also tried them on for me so that I could see what they'd look like. It's such a shame I won't be there to help you put them on for the first time. Others will see them before I do.
Just one little tip. When you take them off, blow in them as they will be slightly damp from wearing.
Looking forward to seeing you wear them on Saturday night, much love,
Ken xxxx.

* * *

The young man got down on his knees and said shyly, "Darling will you marry me?" as he offered her a glittering ring.
"Oh my!" she said, looking pleased. "Are they real diamonds?"
"They'd better be," he replied. "Otherwise I've been cheated out of £15."

* * *

A beggar went up to a well-dressed man and said, "I'm so hungry, I haven't eaten in three days."
"Well, force yourself," came the reply.

* * *

Little William walks past his parent's bedroom one night and spots them making love. The following morning he asks his dad why they were acting in that way.
"It's because your mother wants a baby," replies dad.
A couple of days later, he sees his mother performing oral sex and later asks his dad why she was doing that to him.
"Because she wants a Porsche," replies dad.

* * *

MEN AT DEATH'S DOOR

What do you call a woman who knows where her husband is all the time?
A widow.

* * *

The doctor came out of the consulting room looking very serious.
"I'm sorry, Mrs Powers," he said, shaking his head, "but I'm afraid your husband is at death's door."
"Really!" she replied. "Is it possible to open the door and push him through?"

* * *

A man was lying on his deathbed, and as his life was slipping away, he beckoned his wife to come closer.
"Jenny, darling, I have something to confess. During our married life I was unfaithful to you six times. In fact, I even slept with your best friend. I hope you can forgive me."
"I know exactly what you did," she replied coldly. "Why do you think I poisoned you?"

* * *

It was the day of Charlie's funeral. His wife and two children were sitting in the front row listening to the vicar's sermon.
"...and so, brothers and sisters, we say farewell to Charles, a good and kind man, loving husband, devoted father, always ready to lend a helping hand..."

At that point, the wife, looking slightly shocked, whispered to her eldest son.
"John, quick, we must be at the wrong funeral. Take a peek in the coffin. I don't know who this man is that the vicar is talking about."

* * *

Two women talking over the garden wall.
"So what do you think, Beryl? Would it be fatal if your husband ran away with another woman?"
Beryl thought for a moment. "Yes, it could be. They say the shock of sudden intense happiness can be bad for the heart."

* * *

Following the death of her husband, a woman rang up the local newspaper to put a notice of his death in the obituaries.
"Yes, madam," said the newspaperman, "what would you like to say?"
"John is dead," she replied.
Startled by the abrupt wording, he informed her, "Actually madam, you are allowed up to twelve words for the same price. Is there anything else you'd like to say?"
The woman thought for a moment and then replied,
"John is dead. Set of brand new golf clubs for sale."

* * *

"Jack, it's your brother, Bob, here," came the voice down the telephone line. "I'm not going to be able to get back for dad's funeral because I'm stuck in the outback. Do something nice for him and send me the bill."
So Jack did as his brother wished and sent Bob a bill for £100 which Bob paid immediately.
However, the following month, Bob received another bill for £100 and this happened each and every month. Eventually he managed to catch up with Jack and asked him what was going on.

"Well, you said do something nice for dad," protested Jack, "so I hired him a nice black three-piece suit."

* * *

Our Joan's so kind. She's always thinking of others. When she killed her husband, she used a knife rather than a gun so as not to wake the children!

* * *

Why is it that only 15% of men go to heaven?
If they all went, it would be hell.

* * *

After lying at death's door for more than six weeks, the man made a miraculous recovery. When the doctor told his long-suffering wife, she burst into tears.
"Oh no! What am I going to do now? I sold all his clothes and possessions to pay for the funeral."

* * *

"You know, June, I've been thinking, I'd like to be cremated."
"OK John, I'll just go and get the car."

* * *

Bernard only had minutes to live as he beckoned his wife to come closer.
"Doris, please do one last thing for me, please ride in the same car as my mother on the day of my funeral. Then I can die a happy man."
The wife paused for a moment and then replied,
"Well, all right then, but you know it will completely spoil my whole day."

As the congregation left the church on Sunday morning, the vicar spotted Mrs Jessop.
"Good morning, good morning," he boomed, "and how's your husband?"
"He passed away last week, vicar," she replied.
"Oh, no, how did it happen?"
"He was in the allotment, digging up some potatoes for lunch, when he collapsed and died," she replied.
The vicar looked suitably sombre. "What on earth did you do?" he asked.
"Oh, not to worry, I had a packet of oven chips in the freezer."

* * *

Did you hear about the ex-wife whose husband ran away with his secretary?
Two years later the ex-wife began ringing up her husband's office to be told over and over again that he no longer worked there because he had died.
After a while, the receptionist's curiosity got the better of her and she asked the ex-wife why she kept ringing.
"Oh, I just like to hear you say it," she said bitterly.

* * *

June was dying. She only had a few seconds to live and she called for her husband to come a little closer.
"Fred," she whispered, "when I die I want you to marry Josie from across the street."
"Oh, no," replied her husband shocked, "I don't want to marry anyone after you."
"I insist," she gasped.
"But why?"
"Because I've hated that tart for more than 20 years."

* * *

No woman has ever shot her husband while he's been hoovering.

* * *

An angry woman arrived home from her husband's funeral with his ashes in an urn. She tipped them out onto the table and began speaking to them. "Here, Charles, look at this, it's a beautiful matching set of the finest leather handbag and shoes. Remember? You always promised you'd buy them for me but you never did."
Then she put a pearl necklace on the table.
"And this is the pearl necklace you always promised me - but then, you never kept your promises."
Suddenly she bent down and blew all his ashes on to the kitchen floor. "Well Charles, you'll be pleased to know that's the blow job I always promised you!"

* * *

While his wife was still alive, the husband bought her a headstone engraved with the words "Here lies Doris, cold as usual."
The wife was so angry she immediately went out and got a headstone for him, with the words "In memory of Fred, stiff at last."

* * *

An old man was dying and his wife and family were standing around the bed. He had four tall and handsome blond sons and one small dark-haired boy. In the last few moments of life he beckoned to his wife and whispered,
"Patsy, my life is over, please tell me the truth. Is that small lad, that little one, is he mine?"
"Oh, yes, with my hand on my heart, I swear he is yours."
At that, the man died peacefully with a smile on his face.
"Phew," said the wife to herself, "thank goodness he didn't ask me about the other four."

An old man and a 20-year-old girl got married and for three weeks they were very happy, until one Sunday he collapsed and died.
Her mother arrived to console the unhappy girl.
"Oh, mum," she cried, "it was such a wonderful marriage. We were always so passionate, especially on Sunday when he would make love to the rhythm of the church bells."
The girl suddenly looked thoughtful. "Do you know, I'm sure he'd still be alive today if the fire engine hadn't gone past, clanging its bell so ferociously just minutes before he died."

* * *

It was a huge funeral. Hundreds of women walked solemnly behind Jack's coffin, while up front strode Hilda and her dog, Harvey. A woman from the next village asked someone in the procession what had happened.
"Old Hilda's dog savaged her husband to death," came the reply.
"Oh, really? Do you think it would be possible to borrow the dog?" she asked.
"I expect so, but you'll have to get to the back of the queue."

* * *

Poor old Jake was lying on his death bed with the dutiful family sitting round, when he suddenly roused himself on smelling his wife's cooking in the kitchen. When she saw him open his eyes, she whispered gently to him, "Jake, my poor man, do you have a last wish?"
"Oh, Mary, that I do," he croaked. "May I just have a small piece of that wonderful cake you're cooking in the kitchen?"
"Oh, no," said his wife, "that's for after the funeral."

Bob and Harold had just arrived on the 10th fairway when a funeral procession passed by. Harold stopped playing, put down his golf club and took his hat off.
"That was a nice gesture," remarked Bob.
"Well, it was the least I could do, after all she's been a good wife to me over the past forty years."

* * *

The day of the funeral was wet, windy and very stormy. As the mourners left the graveside, there was a tremendous flash of lightning and a deafening clap of thunder.
"Bloody hell!" cursed the new widow. "It didn't take him long to get up there and start pushing his weight around."

* * *

Said the doctor to the old man,
"I'm sorry, Mr Hodges, you've only got three minutes to live."
"Oh, no!" exclaimed the man. "Is there anything you can do for me?"
"Well, I could get the nurse to boil you an egg."

* * *

An old shop keeper was dying and the family had gathered around his bed. All of a sudden, the old man raised himself up and said:
"Is Jean here?"
"Yes, I am," she replied.
"Is Robert here?"
"Yes, I'm here."
"And is Leonard here?"
"I'm here too."
"Then who the bloody hell is looking after the shop?" he cried.

* * *

There's nothing wrong with my husband that a good funeral wouldn't cure.

* * *

Poor old George. Never out of the betting shop, he was the eternal optimist, believing that one day his boat would come in but it never did. His tips were never any good and he always lost his money. One day, however, his horse almost made third place and the excitement was too much. George dropped dead from a heart attack.
Later that day, Malcolm, an old friend, was asked to go down to the mortuary to identify the body. But when he got there, the attendant had muddled up the labels on the drawers and Malcolm was shown three bodies, not one of them being George.
"Oh dear," sighed Malcolm good naturedly. "Just like George, still unable to get into the first three."

* * *

A long-suffering wife rang up the doctor's one evening and said urgently, "Hello, doctor, my husband's lying at death's door, could you possibly come round and pull him through?"

* * *

The funeral procession made its way down the road, six close members of the family carrying the coffin between them. On top of the coffin was a fishing line, a net and some bait. A passerby remarked, "He must have been a very keen fisherman."
"Oh, he still is," came the reply. "He's off to the river as soon as they've buried his wife."

* * *

MEN AT FATHERHOOD

"Mummy, mummy, what's an orgasm?" asked the little son.
"I don't know, darling," replied mum. "Go and ask your father."

* * *

A group of children were on a school outing when they had to stop to let some of them have a wee. The girls went behind the hedge but it was a very painful experience because the ground was covered in nettles and thistles. Then one little girl looked up and saw a little boy pull his willy out, start to pee, standing there quite unaffected.
"Oooh!" she marvelled. "That's a good thing to bring on a picnic!"

* * *

If a woman has an inferiority complex, there's one sure-fire way of curing it.
Spend a week sick in bed and let the husband look after the house and kids!

* * *

A young couple were admiring their newborn baby son.
"Just look at his pecker," said the husband proudly. "It's absolutely huge."
The wife nodded in agreement and replied sadly, "Never mind darling, at least he's got your eyes."

* * *

"Mummy, mummy, what's that wrinkled thing that grandma keeps talking about?" asked the little girl.
"Don't worry," replied mum, "she's just talking about grandpa."

* * *

A little boy was stood in the middle of a busy high street, crying his eyes out.
"Hello, son," said the policemen, "what's wrong?"
"I've lost my dad," he sobbed.
"Well, what's he like?"
"Beer, cigarettes and women," said the boy.

* * *

On Saturday mornings it was the father's job to take his small daughter to ballet classes and then drive her home afterwards. One Saturday, however, he was unwell so mum took her. When the little girl returned, dad asked her how it went.
"Great," she replied, "and guess what? we didn't see any bastards going or coming back."

* * *

Fathers are embarrassed when their children tell lies, and even more embarrassed when they tell the truth.

* * *

A man had his neighbours round for some beers and decided to show off how well his young five-year-old son was talking.
"David, would you like to say something before you go to bed?" he asked.
"But daddy, I don't know what to say."
"Just repeat what you've heard me say," said dad.
"OK, I wish I hadn't asked that damned prat from number 6."

A man, his wife and young daughter spent a day at the zoo. As they were walking around they came to the elephant enclosure where a huge African elephant was pacing up and down. The young daughter was at an age where she was continually asking questions.
"Mummy, what's that long thing on the elephant?"
"That's its trunk," she replied.
"No, no, at the other end," said the daughter.
"Oh, that's its tail."
"No, mummy, the long thing underneath."
Mum thought for a moment, decided she was too young and replied, "Nothing to bother about, darling."
But as mum walked on, she turned to her dad and asked, pointing, "Daddy, what's that thing under the elephant?"
"That's its penis," replied dad.
"Oh," said the daughter, "mummy told me it wasn't worth bothering about."
"Well, the trouble is I spoil her," he said.

* * *

Children are a great comfort in your old age, and they help you get there faster too.

* * *

"Please miss," said the little boy, "should a person be punished for something they didn't do."
"No, Johnny," replied the teacher.
"Oh thank you, miss," he said, "because I haven't done my homework."

* * *

A father is shouting at his son in exasperation.
"Billy, Billy, just for once, I'd like to go a whole day without shouting at you for your misbehaviour."
The little boy replies, "OK, dad, you have my permission."

"Son, never go anywhere near a whore-house, believe me, it could have fatal results," said the devout father.
But some years later, out on a stag night, he and his mates landed up in the redlight district and before he knew what was happening, he was inside the brothel and upstairs in one of the bedrooms. There laying naked on the bed was an attractive young woman and suddenly his father's long lost words came back to him.
"Oh, no!" he gasped. "My father was right. I can feel myself going stiff already."

* * *

She said she wouldn't mind having a baby, the only drawback being that you have to marry one to get one.

* * *

Did you hear about the poor wife who asked her husband to change their son?
He went missing for five hours and eventually returned with a daughter.

* * *

I really don't want to go to school today, dad," said his pathetic son, "I've got tummy ache."
"I'm sure it'll soon wear off," said dad impatiently.
"But I don't like school, the kids don't like me and neither do the teachers," he cried.
"Now look here, Clive, stop being such a wally. You're 42 years old and the headmaster. You have to go!"

* * *

"Daddy, daddy, can you make a noise like a frog, please?"
"I suppose so, but why do you ask?"
"Because mummy says she can't wait for you to croak."

* * *

A real wally and his pregnant wife were in an ambulance on the way to hospital. The poor woman was in great pain and confessed to her husband that she was very frightened. He put his arm round her and said sympathetically,
"Darling, are you sure you want to go through with this?"

* * *

A father, who had not been feeling well, asked his young son to take his urine sample down to the doctor's surgery. However, on the way, the boy fell over and spilt most of the liquid on the ground, and because he was afriad of his father's anger, he topped it up from a cow in a nearby field. Some days went past, then one evening the father came home looking dazed and shocked. He said to his wife,
"Oh Doreen, we've done it now. You should never have insisted on getting on top. Now I'm going to have a baby!"

* * *

A father walks into his son's room unexpected and says, "Stop that now or you'll end up going blind."
The boy replies, "Well, can't I at least carry on until I need glasses."

* * *

A policeman spotted two men fighting in the street, while close by stood a small boy sobbing and crying out, 'Daddy, daddy'.
"All right, son," said the constable trying to comfort him, "which one's your daddy?"
"That's what they're fighting about," he cried.

When John met up with Colin for their usual weekly game of golf, he was surprised to see that Colin had two caddies with him. Nothing was said but half way round the course, John became so curious he had to know why.
"Colin, how come you've got two caddies with you. It's a bit unusual, isn't it?"
"Well, yes, I suppose it is," replied Colin, "but you see, my wife's been complaining that I don't take the kids out enough."

* * *

Little Tommy went up to his father and asked him where he came from. Now dad had dreaded this day, feeling very embarrassed, but he bravely took up the challenge and went through the whole subject in fine detail. He talked about love, the sexual act and finally the precautions that should be taken. When he had finished he looked at his son and said, "There, I hope that's helped you understand. By the way, what made you ask me today?"
"Well, dad, I was talking to my friend Charlie and he said he came from Devon."

* * *

"Daddy, daddy, is it bad to have a willy?"
"No, son, why do you ask?"
"Because earlier in the bathroom, I saw you trying to pull it off."

* * *

A father and his son both had disabilities. The father had one leg shorter than the other, so he limped, and the son had a stutter. One day, the son said to his dad,
"D.d..d...dad, I...I....I've g...gg.g..got a gr...gr...great idea."
He told his dad that if he walked with one leg in the gutter, he wouldn't limp. So dad did this and got knocked down by a car. Later in the hospital, his son came to visit him.

"S....s....sorry about the a..a...aa...accident, d..d...dad."
"That's all right, son," whispered dad through his bandages. "I've been thinking about your stutter and I've got a good idea."
"G..g...great, dd..d..dad. w..w...what is it?"
"Keep your fucking mouth shut."

* * *

Dad had volunteered to take the Tuesday night scout group. To gain the attention of this unruly group, he decided to puzzle them with a strange question.
"OK boys, anyone who thinks they're stupid, please stand up."
After a moment, one young boy at the back stood up.
"So Matthew, you think you're stupid, do you?"
"No, Mr Hodges, but I didn't like to see you standing there all by yourself."

* * *

A young boy is walking home from school when a car pulls up beside him and a man rolls down the window.
"Hello, let me give you a lift."
"No thanks," says the boy.
A bit further along, the car pulls up again.
"OK, look, I've got some sweets and a magazine you'll like."
"No!" shouts the boy. "Now go away."
But the man persists and draws up again.
"Oh, come on, I'll give you £5 as well."
The boy stops and glares at the man.
"I've had enough!" he shouts. "You bought that bloody Skoda, dad, you're going to have to live with it."

* * *

"Daddy, daddy," said the little boy, watching his father take a shower. "What are those for?"
"FOUR?!" screamed dad.

* * *

It was dad's turn to take his son out for the afternoon.
When they returned, mum asked the little boy if he had enjoyed going to the zoo.
"Oh, yes, mum," he replied "and dad liked it too. He got very excited when one of the animals came racing home at 25/1."

* * *

A man was describing his new secretary to some friends who'd come round for a drink.
"She's punctual, efficient, has the office running like clockwork, and she's very attractive. Yes," he mused, "she's a real doll."
"A doll, daddy?" asked his young daughter. "And does she close her eyes when you lay her down?"

* * *

The Higgins family went on holiday to Norfolk where they rented a cottage by the river. Now the rent was quite cheap because there was no inside toilet. They had to make their way to a hut at the bottom of the garden whenever they felt the urge to go. The eldest son, Harold, soon got bored with his surroundings and in a fit of temper, he threw the small hut over the hedge into the river. Some time later, his dad stormed up to him as he was playing ball on the grass.
"Was it you, you little bugger, that threw the hut into the river?"
"No dad, honest, it wasn't me," he replied.
So dad sat him down and recounted the story about the time George Washington cut down his father's cherry tree.
"Now remember this, son. When George Washington's dad asked

him if he had done it, the boy answered, 'Father I cannot tell a lie, it was me' and because of his honesty, he wasn't punished. So I'll ask you once again, did you throw the hut into the river?"
"Yes, OK, I can't tell a lie, it was me."
With that, his dad belted him one.
"Hey, that's not fair," protested the son. "George Washington didn't get belted."
"No, but when he cut down the cherry tree, his father wasn't sitting in it at the time."

* * *

A father was summoned to his son's university to see the head of faculty.
"I have good news and bad news. Your son's grades have fallen drastically," said the head, "because he has become a blatant homosexual and spends his whole time in the pursuit of pleasure."
"Oh, no!" said the father. "And what's the good news?"
"He's been voted Queen of the May."

* * *

A father was talking to his son on the eve of his son's marriage. He said, "Son, at the beginning it's tri-weekly, then ten years on, it's try weekly, and once your silver wedding anniversary arrives, it's try weakly."

* * *

The family were relaxing on the beach. Mum and dad were sunbathing, their three-year-old daughter was making sandcastles. As the little girl looked up she saw a small boy peeing in the water.
"Daddy, daddy," she said. "I want one of those."
Without opening his eyes, dad replied, "Well, if you're a good girl, I'll get you one later."

What did the little boy say when he passed his parent's bedroom late one night?
"And they sent me to the doctor's for sucking my thumb!"

* * *

"Dad," said the troubled 17-year-old youth, "I keep getting these urges all the time, what should I do?"
"Go and see the doctor," replied his father. "I'm sure he'll be able to help."
So the boy went to see the doctor but the advice he got did him no good whatsoever. Again he talked to his dad and again he was advised to go back to the doctor's. All to no avail.
"Just try once more," advised his dad, "and if there's no improvement, we'll try something else."
Dispirited, the boy made another journey to the doctor's but this time the doctor was out and the door was opened by his wife. When she saw his troubled face, she asked him what was wrong.
"I keep getting these terrible urges," he replied.
"Oh, I see," she said, enlightened. "I think I've got the answer, come with me." She led him by the hand up to her bedroom where she taught him the secrets of the bed.
Later, when the boy returned home, his dad asked him how it went.
"Great!" smiled the boy. "The doctor's wife has got more brains between her legs than the doctor has in his head."

* * *

"Daddy, daddy," said the little girl. "Can a nine-year-old become pregnant?"
"No," said dad.
"Thanks," she said turning round to her friends. "OK boys, let's go on playing the game."

* * *

MEN AT LOVE

"What do I have to give you to get a kiss?" he simpered.
"Chloroform," she replied.

* * *

Three young women agreed to take part in an intimate survey about taking precautions when having sex. The first said she always carried a packet of condoms so that if the opportunity arose, she was always prepared.
The second woman said she always had the pill in her handbag so if she was away from home for any length of time, she had nothing to worry about.
Then the third woman said that her faith forbade her to use any artificial protection.
"So how do you manage should you have an urge for sex?" she was asked.
"Oh, I carry a tin around with me which has a few stones inside."
The questioner looked puzzled.
"I'm sorry, I don't understand, how does that work?"
"Oh, it's quite simple really" she replied, "I get him to stand on the tin and when I hear it start to rattle, I kick it out from under him."

* * *

How does a jerk tell his girlfriend he wants her to be the mother of his children?
"Oh, shit, the johnny's split."

* * *

Two girls were talking in the pub.
"So how did your date go last night?" asked Sharon.
"Oh, I dumped him, he was an animal," replied her friend.
"How come?"
"Well, after the film, I invited him back to my place for coffee and we hadn't been on the sofa more than a few minutes when he put his hand up my skirt."
"Never!"
"Yes, can you believe it! Everyone knows, a gentleman starts with the tits first."

* * *

Why is a man like a snowstorm?
You don't know when it's coming, how many inches there'll be or how long it'll stay.

* * *

What is the similarity between an open-all-night corner-shop and sex with your husband?
The goods don't look very attractive, there's not a lot of variety, and there's a high price to pay but sadly nothing else available at 3am.

* * *

A woman went to court and was granted a divorce on the grounds that her husband's tackle was so big it caused her great distress. Lo and behold, she was back again in court a year later, divorcing her second husband because his was quite the opposite and therefore very unsatisfactory.
As the judge granted the second divorce, he felt it wise to give the woman a stern warning.
"Madam, I do not wish to see you in this court again. We have better things to do than ascertain the right fitting for you."

A husband and wife had a blazing argument over the breakfast table and as the husband stomped off to work, his parting shot was shouted up the garden path.
"And you're no bloody good in bed either."
Later that day he felt very guilty and decided to ring his wife to apologise. It took ages for her to answer and he commented on this when she eventually picked up the phone.
"Oh, I was in bed" she said.
"What! At this time of the day? Why?"
She hesitated for a moment and then replied, "I was getting a second opinion."

* * *

How do you know when a man's had an orgasm?
He's snoring.

* * *

It was a long time since the old man had paid for sex but one Friday night he hobbled along to the local whorehouse and asked the madam how much it would cost.
"£50 for 30 minutes," she replied.
"Bloody hell!" he said surprised. "You're putting me on!"
"That'll be another £20 then," she said.

* * *

A woman went to the doctor's to complain about her husband's poor performance in bed.
"The best thing to do is to tell him exactly what you want," advised the doctor.
So that night in bed she took her husband's hand and put it on her breast.
"Now tell me you love me," she said.
"I love you," he replied.

"Now lower," she whispered.
"I love you," he said gruffly.

* * *

Did you hear about the man who was walking through the woods one night when he stepped on a man's bum?
He heard a girl's voice say, "Thank you".

* * *

The biology teacher asked his class,
"Who can tell me what part of the human body swells to ten times its normal size during moments of high emotion? What about you?" he asked, pointing to a girl on the front row.
"I....er....I can't answer that question," she blurted, "it's too embarrassing."
So he pointed to a boy next to her who replied,
"The pupils of the eye, sir."
"Quite right," said the professor, then turning back to the girl, he said, "Your failure to answer tells me two things. First you were not concentrating during our last lesson, and second that when you get married, you're going to be greatly disappointed."

* * *

The traffic police arrived at the road accident to discover a man and woman having sex on the hard shoulder.
"Hey, you two, what's going on here?"
"Sorry, officer," replied the woman, "I dragged this man out of his damaged car and attempted to give him mouth to mouth resuscitation. Well, one thing led to another..."

* * *

The young bridegroom lay in bed waiting for his new wife to get in beside him.
"How much longer are you going to be?" he asked.
"Quite a while," she said, sitting out on the hotel balcony watching the moonlight glistening on the sea. "My mother said this would be the most wonderful night of my life, and I'm not going to miss it for anyone."

* * *

A young girl said to her dancing partner, "Hey, Darren, I'm ever so hot, let's go outside for a few minutes."
"Oh, Candy," he replied, "do we have to? I like this song."
But she persisted and eventually he gave way. As they slipped out into the dark night, the boy produced a torch from his pocket to light the path.
"Darren, did you have that torch in your pocket when we were inside?" she asked.
"Of course," he replied.
"OK then, let's go back to the dance," she responded sadly.

* * *

What's the difference between a condom and a man?
The condom is no longer so thick and insensitive.

* * *

Why does it take millions of sperm to fertilise one egg?
Because not one of them will stop and ask for directions.

* * *

The marriage counsellor said to the husband, "Did you shrink from lovemaking"
"It's not my fault, I've always been small," he replied.

What is a man's idea of foreplay?
Half an hour of begging.

* * *

Why do male taxi drivers make the worst lovers?
Because they never check to see if you're coming before they pull out.

* * *

The young couple had been married for a month but the bride was still very shy when it came to sex.
Trying to put her at ease, her husband said:
"Darling, when you feel like some love, pull it once. When you don't, pull it 300 times."

* * *

Why do men like love at first sight?
It saves them time.

* * *

"Oh Kevin, don't you think it would be a good idea to make love before we get married?" she said, cuddling up to him.
"Oh no, darling, it won't be long before May," he replied.
"Gosh! how long will it be then?"

* * *

Adam said to Eve, "Do you love me?"
She replied, "Who else?"

* * *

"Sweetheart, do you fancy a quickie?"
"As against what?" she replied.

* * *

As the young couple lay in bed on their wedding night, she whispered to him romantically:
"Will you love me always?"
"Darling, you know I will," he replied. "Which way shall we try first?"

* * *

"A sensible woman should be guided by her head when taking a husband, and by her heart when taking a lover."
Nino de Lenclos

* * *

Two men went on holiday together and each day they would go down to the beach and eye up the beautiful girls. Sadly, only Tom ever picked up a girl, while poor Troy always found himself on his own. On the fifth day, Troy turned to Tom and said:
"What's wrong? Every day I try to get a woman interested in me but they don't want to know."
"Listen, I have an idea," said Tom. "Tomorrow, put a potato down your swimming trunks and walk up and down the beach. That'll soon get them interested."
So Troy did as he was advised, but no matter how often he walked up and down, no one showed the slightest interest. That night he confronted his friend,
"It didn't work, it was all in vain!" he cried in despair.
"But Troy, I've been trying to tell you, next time put the potato down the front of your trunks."

* * *

On their first date she invited him back to her flat for coffee and it wasn't long before they ended up in the bedroom. As they fell onto the bed, he noticed the shelves in her room were stacked high with cuddly toys but in the heat of the moment, forgot all about them. Later, when the ardour had been quenched, he turned arrogantly towards her and said:
"Well, how was it for you then?"
"So, so," she replied. "You can pick something off the bottom shelf."

* * *

"Hey, Jack, what's up?" asked his mate.
"Oh, hello Bob. It's the wife, she's not treating me right. The place is a pigsty, we never have proper meals and most of the time we don't even talk. It's driving me mad. I want a divorce but she won't give me one."
His friend thought for a moment and then said:
"I've heard it said, if you make love to your wife at least ten times a day, you'd end up killing her with love. Then you'll be free - just imagine!"
So with nothing to lose, Jack went home and made love to his wife constantly for the next 12 hours. The following day, he dragged himself to work, barely managed to get through his meetings and arrived home completely knackered. When he got inside the door, he stopped in amazement. The house was spotless, there was a wonderful smell of grilled sirloin steak and his wife was waiting for him in a see-through negligee with a whisky for him in her hand.
"Hello, darling," she cooed. "You see, if you treat me right, then I'll do the same for you."

* * *

A young couple are having drinks in the man's flat. Jake pours Tracy a gin and tonic saying "Tell me when."
"After we've eaten," she replies.

"A man's heart may have a secret sanctuary where only one woman may enter, but it is full of little anterooms which are seldom vacant."
Helen Rowland

* * *

As she lay in bed ready for sleep, her husband brought her a cup of tea and a couple of white tablets.
"What are these?" she asked. "They look like paracetamol."
"That's right," he said.
"But I haven't got a headache."
"Good, then let's get down to it," he smiled, jumping into bed.

* * *

Why is a man like a microwave?
Thirty seconds and he's done.

* * *

Bob was so mean that it surprised his mates to see him taking a woman out to dinner. However, the next day he looked so miserable, they guessed it must have been a failure.
"Hey, Bob, mate, what's wrong?"
"Bloody hell, it cost me a fortune last night. I bought her chocolates, flowers, we went to the best restaurant and I ordered two bottles of champagne, and then we went back to her place."
"Well? Sounds like a winner to me," they said.
"Yes, but a bloke in here has just told me I could have got the same result if I'd bought a couple of drinks and a bag of fish and chips!"

* * *

"Darling, I think black underwear is sexy, it really turns me on."
So she didn't wash his underpants for six months.

A young Scotsman had been courting this girl for more than three months but whenever he took her home, she would never allow him over the doorstep.
"Oh, no, Iain," she would say, "I can see the glint in your eye."
Eventually the Scotsman cottoned on, and on the next date, he wore dark glasses.
"So are you going to invite me in tonight, sweet lassie," he said.
"No, no, Iain," she replied.
"But you can't see the glint in my eye," he persisted.
"No, but I can see the tilt in your kilt!"

* * *

What's the similarity between sex with a wally and a modern injection?
It's all over before you feel a thing.

* * *

A flighty sort of girl married a quiet humble clerk and after a week, things were not going so well.
On the Friday night, he came home from work looking aggrieved and said:
"Jaz, when I got to the office this morning, I discovered a pencil tied to my manhood."
"That's right," she replied, "I thought if you couldn't come, at least you could write."

* * *

A young girl was going out on her first date and knowing this, her mother decided to give her some worldly advice.
"Just remember this, Sharon, towards the end of the evening, he will try to kiss you. But beware, do not be over eager. Then he will try to put his hand on your breasts. It may be nice, but don't let him do it. Of course, he will persist and try and put his hand between your legs. You must say no."

Then she looked at her daughter very seriously and said, "Finally he will try and get on top of you and have his evil way. However much you like it, you must say no. It will bring disgrace to the family."
So the young girl went out on her date and the next day she couldn't wait to tell her mother what had happened.
"I did exactly what you told me to do," she said, "and I never disgraced the family. When he tried to get on top of me, I fought him off, turned him over and got on top of him. Then I disgraced his family."

* * *

A woman went to the doctor feeling unwell and was diagnosed as having a bad heart and being run down.
"You need to have lots of rest and steer clear of cigarettes, alcohol and sex," he said.
A few weeks went by and the woman returned to the surgery.
"Listen, doctor, I'm beginning to feel a little better. Could I just have a cigarette now and again?"
"Well, all right, just two a day."
Another week went by and she returned again.
"Oh doctor, please, please, may I have just a small tot of whisky before I go to bed?"
"OK, but just a very small glass once a day."
Eventually she returned a third time.
"Oh doctor, it's a long time since I've had any sex. Surely there'd be no harm in a little bit now and again?"
The doctor pondered for a moment and replied, "OK, but it must be with your husband. You must not have any excitement."

* * *

Every woman has to love something, even if it is only a man.

* * *

At the local nudist camp, the man said to the girl, "Why do you lower your eyes when I say I love you?"
She replied, "To see if it's true."

* * *

"Is this your first time?" simpered the lovestruck boy.
"Yes, it is...today," she replied.

* * *

"He says his lust is in his heart.
I hope it's a little lower."
Shirley Maclaine

* * *

It was the office Christmas party, the drinks had flowed and everyone was a little the worse for wear. As the night progressed, a couple disappeared into one of the dark unused offices and started making love on the floor.
"Oh, Tony!" cried the girl. "This is wonderful, you've never made love to me like this before."
He replied, "That's probably because I'm not Tony."

* * *

What did the selfish man say to his girlfriend?
"Coming, ready or not."

* * *

Dad had been in bed for a few minutes when he heard his daughter arrive home and disappear with her boyfriend into the front room. For a while he could hear voices, but then it all went quiet, so he thought he'd better go down and check everything was all right.
As he opened the living room door he saw the couple writhing in ecstasy on the floor.
"Well, I never...!" he exclaimed.
"Oh, come off it, dad," said his daughter, quite unflustered, "of course you did, otherwise I wouldn't be here."

* * *

What do you call a man with a 1" willy?
Justin.

* * *

After their honeymoon night, the new husband tripped jauntily down the stairs for breakfast, only to be faced with a lettuce leaf on a plate.
"What's this?" he asked, surprised.
"I was just curious to know if you ate like a rabbit as well," replied his wife.

* * *

As the man was walking down the street, he saw a beautiful girl coming towards him, wearing the tightest pair of jeans he had ever seen on anyone.
"Excuse me, Miss," he enquired, "I hope you don't mind me asking, but how could anyone get into such a tight pair of jeans?"
She replied, "Well, you could start by buying me a glass of wine."

* * *

A man arrived home unexpectedly from work to find his wife in bed with a stranger.
"Explain yourself, Marjorie!" he exclaimed.
"Oh, it's quite simple really, darling," she said. "This poor man came to the door this afternoon, asking for help. He looked so down on his luck that I invited him in for a cup of tea and on seeing the state of his clothes, I rummaged through your wardrobe for anything you no longer used. So he's now got that old pair of green corduroy trousers and your old sports jacket. I've also given him the black pair of shoes that you said were too tight. Then as he was heading for the door, he asked me if there was anything else that my husband didn't use..."

* * *

Did you hear about the stupid man who succeeded in getting a date with a beautiful blonde?
She told him to bring some protection when he came round to her flat, so he turned up with two bodyguards.

* * *

A rich old man woke up one morning and immediately called for his manservant.
"Hobbs, quick, I've got an almighty erection."
"Yes, sir," replied Hobbs, "shall I call your good wife?"
"No, no, man, fetch the car, this was made for the West End."

* * *

What's the difference between a woman and a computer?
No woman would accept a 3.5" floppy.

* * *

War had been declared and Jack Peters was called up for military service. First he had to be examined by the army doctor.
"Mmm," mused the doctor, looking at Jack's naked body, "you're rather small, aren't you?"
Jack replied nervously, "We're only going to fight them, aren't we?"

* * *

"Would you like a nibble of my sausage?"
"Not at the moment, let's eat first."

* * *

A young couple were parked down Lover's Lane, in the throes of passion, when suddenly the man cried out in pain.
"Aah! I can't move!" he yelled. "Something's gone in my back."
The girl rushed to the nearest telephone box and called an ambulance which arrived ten minutes later.
"I think you've slipped a disc," said the paramedic. "We'll have you out of there and more comfortable as soon as we can."
However, it soon became apparent that this was not to be because they couldn't get him out of the car. So they called for the fire brigade who soon realised the only way to get him out was to cut the back of the car off.
Having done this, they gently lifted the poor man out, hiding his embarrassment with a blanket, and soon he was heading for the local hospital. Meanwhile, the poor girl was standing there in floods of tears.
"Don't worry, Miss," said the kindly fire officer. "They'll soon have him sorted out."
"Oh bugger him!" she replied. "What's my husband going to say when he sees the car?"

* * *

"My friend fancies you."
"Well, just keep your friend in his underpants, out of trouble."

* * *

The childless couple had been married for 60 years and were celebrating their wedding anniversary with friends and relatives. At the end of the night, the couple retired to bed, slightly drunk.
"You know, Doris, it's been a great night and it reminds me of when we got married all those years ago."
"Yes, Fred, and do you remember the honeymoon?"
"Oh, yes, we were so young and naive. These days kids of 16 know a lot more about sex than we did."
"I know," she sighed. "I'm sure they wouldn't have had the problems we had on our wedding night." She snuggled closer to her husband and whispered, "Darling, would you like to try again?"

* * *

"Oh, I feel so tired," said the young girl to her friend. "Last night, I didn't sleep till after three."
"Gosh! No wonder you're tired," replied her friend. "Twice is usually all I need."

* * *

Martin was on his way home from work when he came upon a dreadful road accident that had occurred a few minutes earlier. Round the body stood many sobbing women, each one moaning "Bronze is dead, Bronze is dead". There lying on the ground, he saw a gruesome sight. A huge lorry had inflicted unspeakable injuries on a man, not the least of which had severed off his 18" penis.
When he arrived home, he related the incident to his wife, describing the injuries in great detail.
"Oh, no!" she gasped in horror, "Bronze is dead, Bronze is dead."

The 19-year-old daughter said to her mum:
"Did you ever have sex when you were my age?"
"Unfortunately I did," replied mum, "and let that be a lesson to you."
"Why, what happened?"
"I ended up marrying your dad."

* * *

The young man picked up a girl at the night club and took her back to his place. Unbeknown to him, the girl was a nymphomaniac and it wasn't long before she had him in bed performing like an athlete, for hours on end. After the eighth time, he was so exhausted, he excused himself on the pretence that he had to put the dog out.
He donned his shorts, rushed downstairs and out into the night.
"Phew!" he gasped, before peering down into his shorts. But for a moment he couldn't see anything, then he spied it, tiny and shrivelled up.
"There, there," he whispered. "You can come out now, she's not here."

* * *

What's the difference between a husband and boyfriend?
About 50 minutes.

* * *

"I'd go to the ends of the world for you," said the starry-eyed lover.
"Yes, but would you stay there?" she replied.

* * *

What were the first words Eve said to Adam when they met?
"Don't think you're sticking that thing in me."

* * *

MEN AT MEDICINE

An old man goes to the doctor's for a routine check up and while there, he tells him he is getting married again to a 22-year-old girl.
The doctor looks quite concerned and feels he should give the old man some advice.
"You know, Jake, sex with such a young girl could be fatal."
The old man smiled and replied confidently,
"You don't get to my age without a few setbacks, so if she dies, she dies."

* * *

An old man went to the doctor's complaining that he couldn't pee any more.
"I see," said the doctor, "and how old are you?"
"91," he replied.
"Well, don't you think you've peed enough?" he suggested.

* * *

A man went to the doctor's complaining he was disappointing his wife in bed. No matter how hard he tried, his whole performance was over in less than two minutes.
The doctor suggested that at the crucial moment, he should give himself a shock and that would cure the problem. So the man bought a starting pistol on his way home and when he walked in, he found his wife already in bed. They started their lovemaking and at the crucial moment he fired the starting pistol.
Next day he returned to the doctor's.

"How did it go?" asked the doctor.
"Awful, doctor. When I fired the starting pistol, the wife jumped up in shock, hit her head and is in hospital with concussion, and the gas man came out of the wardrobe with his hands in the air."

* * *

Did you hear about the doctor who thought he was God's gift to women?
When he took a female patient's pulse, he always adjusted it downwards to compensate for having touched her!

* * *

A couple went to the doctor's because the man had been complaining of feeling unwell. After a lengthy examination, the doctor left him to get dressed while he spoke to the wife in the other room.
"Your husband is suffering from extreme stress. If he doesn't start to ease the tension, his blood pressure will rise even higher and it could prove fatal. I think you may be able to ease the stress. Make sure he has everything he needs. Always have his meals ready for him, run him a nice hot bath every night, deal with all the household problems yourself and take over all the driving, so he can completely relax."
At that moment the husband appeared and the couple let the surgery.
"So, Mabel, what did the doctor say?" asked the husband.
"You're going to die," she replied.

* * *

The young doctor rushed into the kitchen.
"Julie, quick, give me the keys to the car, I've just had an emergency phone call. A man has rung up saying he can't live without me."
"Hold on a minute," said the wife meekly. "I guess that phone call was for me."

A woman takes her elderly husband to the doctor's for an annual check-up and after a thorough examination gives him a clean bill of health.
"You're in remarkable condition," he says. "What's your secret?"
The old man smiles and replies, "I think I have a fairy godmother looking out for me. Do you know, when I go for a pee in the middle of the night, she turns the light on for me in the bathroom and then when I finish, she turns it off again!"
"Poppycock!" retorts his poor long-suffering wife. "Every night he pees in the refrigerator."

* * *

A man walked into a doctor's surgery, took out his penis and laid it on the desk.
"Look at that, doc," he said.
"Mmmm," remarked the doctor, "what seems to be the problem?"
"Oh, there's no problem; it's just so perfect, I had to show someone."

* * *

A very excited man rang 999.
"Ambulance, please," he shouted. "My wife's having a baby."
"All right," came the reply, "just keep calm. Is this her first baby?"
"Don't be silly!" he exclaimed. "I'm her husband."

* * *

It was Jack's 75th birthday and time for him to have his annual check-up at the doctor's. He asked his wife to come along because his hearing was beginning to falter and he didn't want to miss anything that was said.
After a thorough examination, the doctor sat back in his chair and said,"Just to be on the safe side, I'd like to do some extra tests, so I'll need a urine sample, a stool sample and a sperm sample."

Jack turned to his wife and whispered, "What did he say, Bet?"
"It's OK," she replied, "just leave your underpants here."

* * *

Why is it quicker and easier for psychiatrists to treat a man?
When he's asked to go back to his childhood, he's already there.

* * *

A man rushed into the doctor's surgery, highly agitated, and accosted the receptionist.
"I must see the doctor quickly!" he cried. "I've got something wrong with my willy."
The receptionist was shocked.
"You can't come in here, shouting about things like that, think of the other people waiting. Now I suggest you go out and come in again, this time say you have something wrong with...(she thinks)...your ear."
So the man did as he was told and came in again.
"I have something wrong with my ear," he said.
"Really?" replied the receptionist, "and what exactly is wrong with your ear?"
"I can't piss out of it," he replied.

* * *

"Doctor, I have a small, ugly and embarrassing wart."
"Well, divorce him."

* * *

A woman walks into the doctor's surgery seeking advice about her husband.
"Oh doctor, I think my husband's gone mad," she says.

"Now just calm down," replies the doctor, "and tell me what the symptoms are."
"He thinks he's the boss!"

* * *

Following a thorough examination in the sugery, the grim-faced doctor came out to speak to the patient's wife.
"I'm afraid I don't like the look of your husband," he said.
"Well, neither do I," she replied, "but he's good to the kids."

* * *

Two friends meet up at work.
"You were late this morning, Pete."
"Yeah, I had to go for a paternity test."
"Really? And were you the father?"
"They'll never find out," laughed Pete. "The silly buggers took samples from my finger."

* * *

A very old man went to the doctor's in some distress.
"Oh doctor, please help me," he pleaded, "Every morning at 7 o'clock, I have a good piss and move my bowels."
"Well, that's very good," replied the doctor. "It means you're very regular."
"No, no, doctor, you don't understand. I don't get up until 9 o'clock."

* * *

A woman with twelve kids in tow arrived at the doctor's surgery looking very happy.
"Doctor, I've got some wonderful news. I'll never be pregnant again, thanks to my new instrument."
The doctor looked puzzled.

"New instrument? What's that?"
"It's my hearing aid," she said proudly. "Now I can hear properly."
The doctor still looked puzzled, so she explained further.
"Before I had this, we would get into bed at night and my husband would say 'Shall we go to sleep or what?', and I would say what?"

* * *

A wife came back from the doctor's smiling broadly.
"Guess what the doctor said? I have the body of a 25-year-old."
"Oh yeah!" replied the husband jealously, "and what did he say about your 50-year-old arse?"
"Oh, we didn't have time to mention you."

* * *

A married couple rushed into the dentist's surgery and pleaded to be seen immediately.
"We're on our way to catch a plane," said the husband, "and if we miss it our holiday will be ruined. Please help us, a tooth needs to be pulled as soon as possible. Cost is no problem; forget about the anaesthetic."
"You know, it will be agony without pain killers," warned the dentist.
"Never mind the pain, just do it," the husband said pleadingly.
"OK, I think you're a very brave man, now which tooth are we talking about?"
The man turned to his wife and said, "Quick, Beryl, get up on the seat and show him the tooth."

* * *

A wife goes to the doctor's to pick up her husband's test results, only to find out that he has less than 24 hours to live. She decides not to tell him but is determined to make his last night as pleasurable as possible.

She suggests they go to bed early and when they get into the bedroom, she wears her sexiest negligee and performs the most amazing sex on him before they finally fall asleep. An hour later, the husband wakes up, remembers their wonderful lovemaking - the best they've ever had in the whole of their marriage - and nudges his wife for a repeat performance.
During the night he nudges her every hour and by the time dawn is breaking the poor wife is completely exhausted.
"Hey, Doris, let's do it again," he whispers.
"Enough's enough," she retorts angrily. "It's all right for you, you don't have to get up in the morning."

* * *

A sea captain arrived home after 18 months at sea to discover his wife was pregnant.
"I don't understand," he told the doctor. "How can that be?"
"It's what's known as a 'revenge pregnancy,'" explained the doctor.
"What does that mean?"
"It means someone's had it in for you."

* * *

A young couple were on their honeymoon night. The husband turned to his wife and said, "Am I the first man?"
She replied, "Why am I always asked that question!"

* * *

An old couple arrive at the fertility clinic to tell the doctor they would like another baby.
"Well,well!" exclaimed the doctor. "It might not be too easy at your age. I think we'll need a sperm sample to begin with."
The couple were handed a jar and directed to a nearby cubicle.
Grunts and groans were heard to come from the cubicle but it was

nearly three hours before they reappeared, both red in the face from their exertions.
"Everything all right?" enquired the doctor.
"Not really," replied the man. "First I used my right hand, then I used my left hand, then my wife tried as well, but we still can't unscrew the lid of the jar."

*   *   *

It was the most important medical conference of the year, held on the shore of Lake Geneva and attended by the world's leading specialists in new medical breakthroughs.
Over the two days, a male and female doctor became very attracted towards each other and it wasn't long before they went up to her hotel room.
"Excuse me a moment," she said. "I've just got to wash my hands and then I'll pour us a drink."
Later, after a couple of gin and tonics, they retired to the bedroom and again she excused herself for a moment while she washed her hands.
For a short while they remained passionately entwined and afterwards she again went to wash her hands. On her return, the male doctor remarked, "I bet you're a surgeon."
"Yes, I am," she replied in surprise. "How did you know?"
"Because you're always washing your hands."
She replied, "And I bet you're an anaesthetist."
"Yes! how did you guess?"
"Well, I didn't feel a thing," she said.

*   *   *

The man was celebrating his 102nd birthday. Attending the party was the old man's doctor, who congratulated him on his good health.
"You're in such good shape, physically and mentally, that I won't want to see you again for another year."

"Thank you, doctor, does that mean you think I'll live to see my next birthday?"
"Certainly – it's very rare for people to die between 102 and 103."

* * *

The doctor visited the man at home because he was too sick to get out of bed.
"So, you're no better, Mr Simple, but why haven't you taken any of the medicine I left you?"
"I couldn't," replied Mr Simple. "It says on the label to keep the bottle tightly corked."

* * *

A man goes to the doctor's about his wife.
"Oh, doctor, something dreadful has happened. I've been married to my wife for nearly 25 years, she's always been very loving towards me and we've had a very happy marriage. However, since she came to see you last month with bad headaches, she's changed completely. She doesn't come home, stays out with her bingo friends and never gives me those little treats we used to have. What did you do to her?"
"I didn't do anything much," replied the doctor. "I just advised her to go to the opticians and get a pair of glasses."

* * *

A man wakes up in hospital after an horrific motorway accident.
"Doctor, doctor, help me, I can't feel my legs."
"No, you wouldn't," replies the doctor. "I had to amputate your arms."

* * *

A wife receives a message from the doctor's surgery to say that they've mixed up her husband's test results. He's either got herpes or a severe heart condition.
"Well, what shall I do?" she asks in despair.
"We would suggest you send him out jogging and if he comes back, then sleep in separate beds."

MEN AT MARRIAGE

Janet arrived at her neighbour's house for their weekly get-together. As she walked in, she exclaimed with delight, "Oh Doris! What beautiful flowers! Who sent them to you?"
"My husband," she replied.
"Oh, you are lucky. What do you have to do for them?"
"I have to spend the whole weekend with my legs in the air," she said, looking annoyed.
"Really!" exclaimed Janet. "Haven't you got a vase?"

* * *

"It's no good," said the tearful girl to her friend. "I'm leaving him tonight, it's this awful drinking."
"But you've only been married three weeks. Why did you marry him in the first place if he drinks so much?" asked the friend.
"But I didn't know he drank until one night he came home sober," she replied.

* * *

The woman's husband had been missing for three months. No one had any idea what had happened to him. He'd just walked out of the house one day and disappeared.
Then the woman received a call from the coroner's office asking her to go to the morgue to identify a body.
The attendant pulled back the sheet to reveal a well-endowed corpse.
"No," said the woman, "that's not my husband, but some woman has lost a very good friend."

The woman said to her friend, "My husband is no good."
"But," protested her friend, "you told me he was a model husband."
"That's right, he is a model husband, but not a working model."

* * *

Martha and her friends from bingo went to Blackpool for the day and after lunch she was persuaded to visit Gypsy Lil, the famous fortune teller. After having her palm crossed with silver, Gypsy Lil looked into the crystal ball and gasped with horror.
"I'm afraid I have some bad news to tell you," she said. "Prepare yourself for the worst. Your husband is going to meet a violent death."
"Oh dear," replied Martha. "Will I be found guilty?"

* * *

A passenger plane has gone out of control and is plummeting to earth. One of the stewardesses rushes into the cockpit and says to the handsome pilot:
"Captain, please make me feel like a woman once more before I die."
"OK," he says, ripping off his shirt. "Iron this for me."

* * *

The solicitor was reading out the last will and testament of Hilda Blackthroat. After informing the close relatives about the contents, he came to the final paragraph.
It said, "And don't think that I've forgotten my husband, Frank. So hello there, Frank."

* * *

"But I don't understand why you say you have nothing to live for?" asked the puzzled wife. "There's all sorts of things. The house isn't paid for, the car isn't paid for, there's the bank loan, the school fees..."

The minister and his new wife were on their honeymoon. While the minister went into the bathroom to prepare himself, his bride slipped into bed.
"Darling," he said, coming back out, "I thought I would find you on your knees."
"Well, if you insist," she replied. "But it's not my favourite position; it gives me hiccoughs."

* * *

"Hello, is that the police station?"
"Yes, how may I help you?"
"Have any mad women escaped from the lunatic asylum recently."
"No, madam, why do you ask?"
"Because someone's run off with my old man."

* * *

The bride and her best friend were discussing the impending wedding.
"Now, don't forget," advised her friend. "If you want a night to remember, get him to eat a dozen oysters beforehand."
Some time later, the two friends met up and the new bride was asked how it went.
"Well, thanks for your advice," she said. "Unfortunately, only eight of them worked."

* * *

Why are married women heavier than single women?
When single women arrive home, they look to see what's in the fridge and go to bed. When married women come home, they see what's in bed and go to the fridge.

* * *

The day before she was married, her mother took the young girl aside and said, "Well, sweetheart, you'll look back on this day as the happiest day of your life."
"But mum, it's tomorrow that I'm getting married," she protested.
"I know, my love, I know."

* * *

"What's wrong Sharon?" asked her concerned friend, "Why are you crying?"
"Oh, Kate, I've had a dreadful row with my old man," she replied. "He stormed out saying he wouldn't speak to me for a whole week."
"Well, enjoy it while it lasts," replied Kate, "a nice bit of peace and quiet."
"That's just the trouble," sobbed Sharon. "Today's the last day."

* * *

After ecstasy, the laundry.
Zen statement

* * *

A man walked into the police station to report the disappearance of his wife. Having taken down the details, the desk sergeant said cheerfully, "Don't worry, sir, we'll find her. Is there any message you'd like us to give her?"
"Just one," he replied. "Please tell her my mother decided not to come after all."

* * *

"The main problem in marriage is that, for a man, sex is a hunger - like eating. If a man is hungry and can't get to a fancy restaurant, he'll go to a hot-dog stand. For a woman, what's important is love and romance."
Joan Fontaine

Watching his wife ironing her bra, the husband said nastily, "I don't know why you bother, it's not as if you've got anything worth holding up."
She replied calmly, "For the same reason I iron your pants."

* * *

Mrs O'Donnell went into the fire station to report her husband was missing.
"I'm sorry, luv," said the fire chief. "You need the police station. They'll be able to help you."
"Not on your nelly!" she replied heatedly. "Last time he went missing, I reported him to the police and they went and found him."

* * *

Marriage is a way of finding out what kind of man your wife would have preferred.

* * *

The husband and wife were having one of their frequent arguments.
"You married me for better or worse!" bellowed the husband as he stormed from the room.
"That was six years ago," she retorted. "I want to know when it's going to get better."

* * *

What do you do when your dishwasher stops working?
Kick him in the balls.

* * *

A woman and her uncouth husband of 20 years were strolling through the park when all of a sudden, he tripped and fell headlong into the wishing well.

For a moment, the woman stood stock still in amazement and then muttered to herself:
"I didn't really think that well would work."

* * *

Two ladies talking over the garden wall.
"Hey, Maureen, that's a nice locket you have there."
"Oh, yes," replied Maureen, "a locket of my old man's hair."
"But he's still alive!"
"He is, but his hair's been gone a long time."

* * *

Another two women talking over the garden wall.
"I never made love to my husband before we got married. How about you?"
"I don't know," replied the second woman. "What's his name?"

* * *

"How can I choose a husband when I can't even decide what to wear!"
Beth Jaykus

* * *

It's called bigamy if you marry two men, but monotony if you marry one.

* * *

"Oh, darling, I felt like a new man when we came back from our honeymoon," he said.
She replied, "So did I."

* * *

"Before marriage, a man declares he would lay down his life to serve you; after marriage, he won't even lay down his paper to talk to you."
Helen Rowland

* * *

"Oh darling," whispered the man seductively, "I'd like to explore parts I've never been before."
"Then why don't you try the kitchen?" she retorted.

* * *

How can you stop a man from wanting sex all the time?
Marry him.

* * *

A couple are celebrating their golden wedding anniversary when the husband notices his wife is quietly crying.
"What's wrong darling? Is it because of this wonderful occasion?"
"No," she replies, "I was just thinking that 50 years ago yesterday, I was still a free woman."

* * *

The husband shouted, "Are you telling me you had half a dozen marriage proposals?"
"Yes," replied his wife.
"Bloody hell, I wish you'd married the first silly bugger who asked you."
"I did," she lamented. "The others tried to change my mind."

* * *

A man kissed his wife goodbye and set off for the office in his car. But he hadn't travelled far before realising he'd left some important papers behind, so he turned round and went back home.
As he entered the kitchen, he saw his wife still in her sheer nightie, bending over the fridge, and in a moment of passion, he took her from behind.
When they had finished, he gave her a sharp smack on the bum.
"Hey!" she said crossly, "what was that for? I submit to your wishes and that's the way you thank me!"
He quickly replied, "That was for not looking round to see who it was."

* * *

Two women talking on the top of a bus.
"Hey, Beryl, has your old man been circumcised?"
"No," replied the other, "he's always been a complete dick."

* * *

"Look at that," said the disgruntled man, peering through the curtains, "every morning when Mr brown leaves the house, his wife always kisses him goodbye. Why can't you do that?"
"Because I don't know him well enough," she replied.

* * *

A small boy, watching his mother washing up, commented, "Mum, where did you work before you got the job with us?"

* * *

A fireman arrives home early from his shift and finds his wife has gone to bed. So as not to wake her, he undresses in the dark and crawls into bed.
"Oh, Rob," she cries on hearing him, "I didn't expect you home yet

but now you're here, can you pop down the all-night shop and get me some pain killers - my head is very bad tonight."
So the husband climbs back into his clothes and makes his way to the shop.
"Hello, Rob," says the shop assistant, "I see you've changed jobs."
"What do you mean?" asked Rob.
"Well, I know you used to be a fireman, but I see you're wearing a policeman's uniform now!"

* * *

"I've just had a really unusual birthday present from my wife."
"Really?"
"Yes, she let me win an argument."

* * *

As the honeymoon couple arrive at the hotel, she turns to her husband and says:
"I don't think I can face all the remarks we're going to get; is there some way we can pretend we've been married for ages?"
"Of course, darling. You carry the bags," he replies.

* * *

If men were the great lovers they think they are, women wouldn't have time for anything else.

* * *

"Doctor, may I have some more sleeping tablets for my husband?"
"Is he still having trouble sleeping?"
"No, he's woken up."

* * *

Two women talking on the top deck of a bus.
"So, Patty, what did you do last night?"
"Well, Jack went down the pub, so I cheered myself up by playing our wedding video backwards. That way I can see myself walk out of the church a free woman."

* * *

The marriage counsellor turned to the couple and asked, "Are your relations pleasant?"
The wife replied, "Mine are, his are dreadful."

* * *

A husband is a lover whose face is unshaved, pants unpressed and stomach out of order.

* * *

"Darling, how shall we celebrate our golden wedding anniversary?" he asked.
"How about a one-minute silence?" she replied.

* * *

A woman went into the police station to report her husband had gone missing.
"He's ruggedly handsome, with blond hair, blue eyes, 6'3" and 35 years old," she told the desk sergeant.
"Hold on, Mabel," he replied, "I know your husband and he's 50, fat and balding."
"I know," she said exasperated, "but I don't want him back."

* * *

Many a woman thinks she can do nothing without a husband, and when she gets one she finds she can do nothing with him.

* * *

"When I see your father standing at the door, I sometimes wish I had loved and lost," she said to her husband sadly.

* * *

What are the ups and downs of marriage?
The toilet seat is always up and his interest is always down.

* * *

Marriage begins as you sink in his arms and ends with your arms in the sink.

* * *

Having read a sex manual on the way home from work, the husband said to his wife over the dinner table:
"I've got a great idea, let's try different positions."
"OK," she replied, "I'll lie on the couch and you can stand at the kitchen sink."

* * *

The old man was sitting in the best chair again, smoking his pipe, constantly belching and forever changing channels on the TV.
After a couple of months of this, the new bride turned to her husband and said:
"John, it's no good. We never have any time to ourselves. I think your father ought to go home."
"My father!" he exclaimed. "I thought he was yours."

It's a fact that single women often claim all the good men are married. Yet married women, more often than not, have nothing nice to say about their husbands.
So the truth is obvious. There's no such thing as a good man.

* * *

My husband used to be an all-round athlete - now he's just all round.

* * *

Girls! If you want to drive your husband mad, smile in your sleep.

* * *

Some husbands come in handy around the house. Others come in unexpectedly.

* * *

"Do you talk to your husband when making love?"
"Only if he rings up."

* * *

The very first time Jean set eyes on her husband, he was picking his teeth outside a second-hand shop. Then he went in and bought them.

* * *

"You lazy, no-good bitch!" shouted the man, "If you got off your arse more and spent some time in the kitchen, we wouldn't need a cook."
"Oh yeah!" she screamed, "If you were better in the bedroom, we wouldn't need the gardener."

* * *

She wrote a letter to her husband:

Jack, I missed you this morning. Won't you come home and let me have another shot? Carol.

* * *

"My husband and I were very happy for 30 years."
"What went wrong?"
"We met."

* * *

Most marriages are very happy. It's living together afterwards that's the problem.

* * *

What's the greatest thing that marriage teaches women?
Patience.

* * *

"So Doris, what have you got in common with your husband?"
"We were both married on the same day," she replied.

* * *

He said to his wife, "Everybody hates me."
"Oh, come on," she replied, "everybody hasn't met you yet."

* * *

"Marrying a man is like buying something you've been admiring for a long time in a shop window. You may love it when you get it home, but it doesn't always go with everything else in the house."
Jean Kerr

He said to his mate, "Is it possible for a man to make a fool of himself and not know?"
"Not if he has a wife," came the reply.

* * *

"If you want to sacrifice the admiration of many men for the criticism of one, go ahead, get married."
Katharine Hepburn

* * *

Said Joan to her neighbour:
"When we were first married, we got on so well, but as we left the church..."

* * *

She had been married so many years, she even faked the foreplay!

* * *

My husband can brighten up a room just by leaving it.

* * *

Said the unhappy wife to her friend:
"Look, Tracy, those curtains over there remind me of my husband."
"Why's that?"
"Neither of them are well hung."

* * *

There's only one thing worse than a husband who never comes home, and that's a husband who hangs around the house all the time.

A woman comes out of court, having just endured a gruelling divorce settlement and as she takes a deep breath of fresh air, she mutters to herself:
"It's about time my luck changed."
All of a sudden, a genie appeared and spoke to her.
"Madam, I am the genie of the air and I grant you three wishes. But please take care with your wishes because whatever you get, your husband will get double.
"I'd like to look ten years younger," she said.
"OK, your wish is granted but remember your ex-husband is now 20 years younger."
"OK, I'd also like to have £1 million."
"Your wish is granted, and your ex now has £2 million. What is your last wish?"
"I'd like to be knocked over by a car and half killed."

* * *

"Mummy, mummy," asked the little girl, "why do fairy tales always begin 'Once upon a time'?"
"Well, that's not quite right, darling," she replied. "Some start 'Sorry I'm late, had to work longer at the office'........."

* * *

Marriage is a partnership where no matter how good a husband is, his wife is still the better half.

* * *

MEN AT PLAY

What's the similarity between electric train sets and breasts?
They're both intended for children, but men always end up playing with them.

* * *

Why is making love to a man like watching a TV thriller?
Just as it gets to the best bit, it's over until the following night.

* * *

It was the grand summer ball and the young debutante was having trouble with her partner. He kept standing on her toes. After the sixth time of this happening, he turned to her and said, "I'm sorry, I'm a little stiff from rugby."
She replied, "I don't care where you're from, just don't keep standing on my feet!"

* * *

"I've got a great idea," said the excited husband. "Let's go out and have some fun."
"OK," replied his wife enthusiastically, "but if you get home before me, don't bolt the door."

* * *

In the middle of the film a woman suddenly stood up screaming and fled into the foyer to complain to the manager that she had been molested.

"Now, now, madam, I'm sure you're mistaken," said the manager, but when another three women also appeared with the same complaint, he realised he had to investigate further. Shining his torch along line three he discovered a man on his hands and knees moving slowly along the seats. He grabbed him by the scuff of the neck and propelled him outside.
"What the hell are you up to?" the manager shouted.
The man looked surprised: "Listen mate, I was on the balcony when I leant over and lost my toupee. I came down to find it and had my hand on it four times but it kept getting away."

* * *

Two women talking.
"Oh Jean, something awful happened this morning. I feel dreadful."
"How come?"
"Our Jack came back really drunk last night, it's a wonder he knew where he was. Anyway, this morning he woke up, handed me £100 and said thanks."
"Listen, don't fret," comforted her friend, "it doesn't mean anything. He just wanted you to get something nice for yourself, I expect."
"No, no," wailed the woman, "you don't understand. Without thinking, I gave him £20 change."

* * *

It was the works outing and six coaches full of employees and their wives headed off towards Blackpool. They all had a marvellous time. Great enjoyment in the amusement park, fun on the beach, plenty of beer at lunchtime and snoozing on the beach again in the afternoon. By evening time most of the wives went to see a show, while the men ended up back in the pub. At midnight, they all got back on the coaches for home. But an hour into the journey, the men were dying for a pee, having drunk so much beer.
"Sorry men," said the bus driver, "there's nothing open this time of night, you'll have to hold on."

But after another 30 minutes, the men couldn't wait any longer, so they urged the driver to pull up at the side of the road and, not caring who saw them, they tumbled off the bus and relieved themselves.
The following morning, Bill woke up with a thumping headache and an angry wife.
"Well, you all certainly acted like animals last night," she said accusingly. "You disappear all evening, come back stinking of beer and then, in front of all those women, flash yourselves as if you didn't have a care in the world." She stopped talking and then smiled: "Mind you, I was very proud of yours."

* * *

A man sat down in a restaurant and ordered his meal.
"A rump steak, chips, mushrooms, tomatoes and peas, please."
"I'm sorry, sir," replied the waiter, "we have no mushrooms at the moment."
"OK, I'll have rump steak, roast potatoes, carrots and mushrooms."
"As I said, sir, we have no mushrooms today."
"Well, in that case, I'll have chicken, chips and mushrooms, please."
"Excuse me, sir," said the exasperated waiter, "how do you spell man, as in management?"
"M A N," replied the man, sounding puzzled.
"And how do you spell dim, as in condiment?"
"D I M," replied the man.
"And finally, how do you spell fuck, as in mushrooms?"
"But there is no fuck in mushrooms," protested the man.
"Exactly, sir," said the waiter, triumphantly. "That's what I've been trying to tell you for the past five minutes, you stupid sod."

* * *

A little old lady knocked at the door of the bikers' club and asked to see the gang leader.
"I'd like to join the bikers' club," she said.

Amused at the sight of this little old lady, the leader replied, "Well, ma'am, we do have to ask our prospective members certain questions to see if they are eligible."
"OK son, fire away," she said.
"Do you have a bike?"
"Sure do," and she pointed to a gleaming Triumph, parked outside the front door.
"Do you smoke and drink?"
"Yep, three packets a day and a bottle of rum."
The biker was very impressed.
He continued, "Have you even been picked up by the fuzz?"
"No," she answered downcast, "but I have been swung round by the nipples on a number of occasions!"

* * *

Two dumb sergeants have 24-hour passes, so they go into town to sup some beer and find some women. Inevitably, they land up at a very sleazy dive, pick up a prostitute and go back to her place.
"I must warn you," she says, "that I have gonorrhoea".
Neither of the two sergeants knows what this is, so one of them goes off and looks it up in the dictionary. A few moments later he returns smiling, "It's all right, no problem."
A couple of weeks go by and the two men experience the same discomforting symptoms. Both have to go and see the medical officer.
"I thought you checked out the word in the dictionary," says one sergeant to the other.
"I did, I thought it was OK."
"Why, what did it say?"
"It said, gonorrhoea is a disease of the privates."

* * *

A man walked into a restaurant and asked for the special of the day, which was hot chilli.
"I'm sorry, sir," replied the waitress, "the man on the next table has just had the last bowl."
So he decided not to eat and had a cup of tea instead.
However, after a while, he noticed the man on the next table had eaten a plate of food and left the chilli untouched.
"Excuse me," he said, leaning over, "if you're not going to eat the chilli, would you mind if I had it?"
"Not at all," replied his neighbour.
So having regained his appetite, the man tucked in with relish but half way down the bowl, he noticed a dead rat lying at the bottom. A great wave of nausea came over him and he puked the chilli he had eaten, back into the bowl.
On seeing this, the man sitting next to him remarked, "Hey, that's as far as I got too."

* * *

Two girls are in the cinema when one turns to the other and says, "Oh Carol, it's horrible, the man next to me is masturbating."
"Just ignore him," advised her friend.
"I can't," she wailed, "he's using my hand."

* * *

A little girl and a little boy lived next door to each other and often played together. However, sometimes they fell out. One day the little boy wouldn't let the little girl play with his football, saying it was just for boys, so she ran crying to her mum. Lo and behold, the next day she came out with her own football, which made the little boy angry. So angry, in fact, that he stopped her playing in his sandpit.
"Ha, ha," he said nastily, "sandpits are just for boys, so there!"
Again the little girl ran crying to her mum and very soon after, a brand new sandpit appeared in her garden. The little boy was fuming. He

pulled down his pants and said angrily, "Only boys have one of these and it's no good going to your mum to get one."
But the little girl ignored him and ran inside.
Some time later, she reappeared smiling, went over to the little boy, lifted her dress and said, "My mum says as long as I have one of these, I can get as many of those as I want, so there!"

* * *

"Hi, I'm a musician. I'm famous for what I can do with my little piccolo."
"That's nice. Did you say you were a musician as well?"

* * *

A man decides to go walking in the country for the day and comes across a large hole in the ground. Curious to know how deep it is, he throws a pebble down but doesn't hear it hit the bottom. So he throws in a larger stone but still no sound. And an even larger stone follows, but he doesn't hear a thing.
Determined not to be beaten, he looks around and spots a big boulder which he just manages to pick up and hurl down the hole. As he waits for a thud, he hears the sound of galloping behind him and just gets out of the way in time, before a goat charges past him into the hole.
Some time later, the man meets a local farmer who asks him if he has seen a goat.
Unable to break the bad news, the man says he hasn't.
"How odd," muses the farmer. "He can't have gone far; I had him tethered to a big boulder."

* * *

Gerald, rich but without much "upstairs", went on his first hunting trip through the wilds of the Australian outback. Momentarily parted from his fellow hunters, he came across a clearing in the

wood and there on the ground was a beautiful naked girl, lying in a very suggestive pose.
"I say," he said, hardly believing his luck, "are you game?"
"Yes," she murmured softly.
So he shot her.

* * *

The wealthy old man strode into the best restaurant in town, with a beautiful girl on his arm. They had cocktails at the bar before sitting down for dinner.
"I'll start with the pate de foie gras, then fillet steak with all the trimmings, followed by chocolate gateau, coffee and mints. Oh, and a bottle of your best champagne," she said.
The old man looked at her quizzically.
"Do you always have such a big appetite?" he asked.
"Only when someone's trying to get into my knickers" she replied sweetly.

MEN AT SENILITY

What do old men and old records have in common?
They both scratch a lot.

* * *

Grandpa was sitting in the garden watching his grandson at play. Little Matthew was digging in the soil when suddenly he pulled out a long wriggling worm.
"Bet you can't put that back in the hole it just came out of," laughed grandpa.
"Oh, I can, I can," he said, "How much will you give me if I do it?"
"20p," said grandpa.
"OK, just give me 15 minutes and I'll show you."
So 15 minutes later, the little boy appeared with the worm, which was now as stiff as a board, and threaded it back in the hole. Grandpa was amazed, but he handed over the 20p and asked little Matthew how it was done. So the young boy explained that he had sprayed the worm with hair spray, which had dried on the worm making it stiff and hard.
A couple of days later, grandpa came round to visit his grandchild again and handed him another 20p.
"But grandpa, you've already given me 20p," said the honest little boy.
"I know, lad," replied grandpa, smiling. "This 20p is from your grandma."

* * *

Why are men and old age alike?
They both come too soon.

* * *

Three old ladies were walking through the park when they were confronted by a man who flashed at them.
Two of them had strokes but the third wasn't fast enough.

* * *

Three old men are sitting in the pub, having their daily pint of beer.
"It's bloody awful getting old," says the first man. "This morning it took me five minutes to remember the wife's name."
The second man nods his head in agreement.
"Aye, bloody terrible. I was sitting at the breakfast table this morning and I couldn't remember if I'd had my breakfast or was still waiting for it."
The third man smiles at his two friends sympathetically.
"Well lads, my memory hasn't failed me yet, touch wood," and he gives the table a sharp knock, only to look at them a moment later and say "Who's there?"

* * *

A sign of old age is when you feel like the morning after the night before - and you haven't even been anywhere.

* * *

An old man passed a young boy sitting on a park bench, crying inconsolably. He sat down next to him and asked, "What's up, young fella, why are you crying?"
The young boy sobbed, "It's because I can't do what the big boys do."
And the old man started crying too.

Because of the restrictions on smoking, two old women used to meet in the park every morning for a good gossip and a couple of fags.
One morning it started to rain, so one of the old women rummaged around in her handbag and came up with a condom which she put over the cigarette to stop it from getting wet.
"What a great idea!" exclaimed the other woman, "Where can I get one of those?"
"Next time you're in town, just pop into the chemist's," she replied.
So the following afternoon, the old woman went into the chemist's shop and asked for some condoms.
Slightly surprised at the old woman's request, he asked, "Yes madam, what size would you like?"
The old woman thought for a moment or two and then said, "One that will go over a camel."

* * *

An old man went along to the local brothel and knocked on the door, which was opened by the madam.
"Hello!" she exclaimed, "What do you want?"
"I want me a woman," he replied.
"Hold on, how old are you?" she asked.
"95," he replied.
"What! Oh, no, you've had it," she said.
"Aaggh," he moaned, taking out his wallet. "How much do I owe you?"

* * *

Two women talking over the garden fence.
One says, "Don't you mind your Alf whistling at all the women as they go by?"
"No," replies the other, "it's just the same as watching dogs chase cars. They never catch them."

* * *

Sitting in the park was the oldest, wrinkliest, frailest man the reporter had ever seen. This could be a good story, he thought to himself, so he went over and engaged the man in conversation.
"So do you think a special diet contributes towards a long life?" he asked.
"Oh, yes," replied the man, "look at me, I smoke five packs of cigarettes a day, drink at least 15 whisky chasers every night and eat three big meals – a big fried breakfast, down the chippie every lunchtime and in the evenings, my favourite food is pork belly with lots of fat oozing and plenty of crackling, or plenty of pies and dumplings."
The reporter was dumbstruck.
"And can I ask how old you are?" he said.
"Yes, I'm 31."

* * *

A man is getting old when the gleam in his eye is merely the sun reflected in his glasses.

* * *

An old man sat staring at his manhood. With a big sigh, he said, "So, my friend, here we are. We were born together, we grew up together and we married together. But now, please tell me, why, after all these years did you have to die before me."

* * *

Two women were in the kitchen listening to their menfolk talk about football and sex.
"Isn't it amazing that at their ages, all they talk about is football and sex?" remarked one.
"Oh, I don't know," replied the other, "at their ages all they can do is talk about it."

* * *

Old Patrick McCassidy was nearly 90 years old but still managed to go to confession every Saturday morning, even though it took him 15 minutes to struggle up the aisle.
This particular Saturday, he went into the confessional and said:
"Forgive me, Father, for I have sinned. I committed adultery with an 18-year-old lassie."
The priest could hardly believe his ears.
"My goodness!" he exclaimed. "When did this happen?"
"About 60 years ago, Father, but I felt like cheering myself up with some nice thoughts."

* * *

Old Sarah, partially deaf and going blind, had been bedridden for two weeks. One morning she received a visitor and after he'd gone, commented to her daughter how much she appreciated the vicar's call.
"Oh, no, mum," said the daughter, "that was the doctor."
"Oh really?" she said disappointed. "I thought he was being rather familiar."

* * *

A very old man walked into his local and ordered a half of mild.
"There you are, George," said the barman. "I haven't seen you around for a while, have you been away?"
"I suppose you could say I have," replied the old man. "As a matter of fact, I've been in jail."
"Jail! Never!" exclaimed the barman. "How come?"
"A month ago, I left here and was walking home when suddenly this young girl appears with a policeman and accuses me of indecent assault. Well, I was so flattered, I admitted it."

* * *

The old man hobbled into the doctor's surgery and said agitatedly, "Oh, doctor, you've got to do something to lower my sex drive."
"Now just a moment, Mr Craddock," he replied. "It's all in your head, you know."
"Exactly!" he exclaimed. "That's what I mean; you've got to lower it a bit."

* * *

Beryl loved her old grandfather very much and knowing he had only a few more years to live, she decided to buy him a very special pet to keep him company.
She arrived at the pet shop, looked at all the animals on offer and finally chose a beautiful green parrot.
"That'll be £1,500," said the shop owner.
"What!" she exclaimed. "That was rather more than I expected to spend."
"But it's a very special bird, madam; it will talk to you intelligently for hours on end."
Finally Beryl was persuaded and she arranged for the bird to be sent round to her grandfather's house.
Some days later, she rang him up to ask how he liked the bird.
"Oh, thank you, my dear," he said. "It was delicious."

* * *

The old man of 78 was getting married again, to a 20-year-old girl, so he went to the doctor's for a final check-up. When he explained the circumstances, he received a cautious response.
"Well, for a man of your age, you're in excellent condition but if you want a successful and peaceful marriage, it may be wise to take in a lodger."
The old man thought about it for a moment and then agreed.
It was almost two years before the doctor saw him again.
"How's it going?" he asked.

"Very well, thank you doctor; in fact, you ought to congratulate me; my wife's pregnant."
"I see," replied the doctor. "So you heeded my advice and took in a lodger?"
"Indeed," answered the old man, smiling. "The lodger's pregnant as well."

* * *

A young man is walking through the park when he sees an old man sitting on a park bench, crying his eyes out.
"What's wrong, are you OK?" he asks.
"No" sobs the old man. "It's my birthday today. I'm 79-years-old and I got married last week."
"Well, that sounds great, you should be really happy."
"I am. My wife is wonderful. She's 25 and the prettiest girl in town."
"Aah" says the man sympathetically. "I guess you may be having some trouble in bed?"
"Oh, no, we enjoy great sex, that's no problem."
"Then I can't see what's wrong. It all sounds ideal to me. Why are you crying?"
"I can't remember where I live."

* * *

An old couple were in bed.
"Quick, Arthur," said the wife. "Put your teeth in; I'm all yours tonight."

* * *

An old married couple were making love in bed when he asked her:
"Doris, am I hurting you?"
"No," she replied. "Why do you ask?"
"I thought I felt you move," he answered.

Two old ladies were visiting the Roman Room at the British Museum. The centrepiece was a magnificent statue of a Roman God, naked except for a fig leaf. Maud wandered on but suddenly realised that Alice was no longer with her.
"Hey, Alice!" she called, spotting her friend standing beneath the great statue. "Come on, what are you waiting for, Christmas?"
"No," she replied, "just autumn."

* * *

MEN AT SIMPLE-MINDEDNESS

"I require only three things of a man. He must be handsome, ruthless and stupid."
Dorothy Parker

* * *

Why do men like clever women?
Opposites attract.

* * *

Why do most men prefer looks to brains?
Most men see more clearly than they think.

* * *

The phone rang for the fourth time that night and the husband picked it up in a rage. He listened for a moment and then bellowed, "How the bloody hell would I know? You want the weather centre, you berk."
"Who was that, darling?" asked his wife, innocently.
"I don't know, some twerp asking if the coast was clear. Bloody pest, that's the fourth time tonight."

* * *

"Hey, Charlie," said one of his mates, "you should go on the stage; those jokes you tell really lift our spirits."
"Oh, no, I couldn't," he replied, "People would laugh at me."

A man was kneeling down, praying to God.
"Oh, Lord, thank you for giving me such a wonderful wife. Why did you make her such a good cook and housekeeper?"
"So you could love her," replied God.
"Thank you, dear Lord, and why did you make her so beautiful and young looking?"
"So you could love her."
The man smiled. "And why did you make her so kind and affectionate towards me?"
"So you could love her."
"And just one more question, Lord, why did you make her so stupid?"
"So she could love you."

* * *

Three scaffolders were moaning about their lunchboxes. The first one, a Welshman, said to the other two:
"If I have Welsh rarebit and leek sandwiches one more time, I swear, I'll jump off this ledge."
The Italian looked at his box and responded:
"Yes, it is right, if I have to eat any more anchovy pizza, I will follow you off the ledge."
Then the third man, an Irishman said, "Well now, be Jesus, if I have to face any more boiled ham and cabbage soup, count me in, lads."
So the next day, lunchtime came and the three men opened their boxes.
"Aaggh," gasped the Welshman, "leeks again" and he jumped from the ledge.
"Mama mia," cried the Italian, "pizza, pizza, pizza" and he jumped from the ledge as well.
The Irishman opened his box, saw the soup, crossed himself and followed his two mates off the ledge.
Some time later, the three wives arrived at the site to be told the dreadful news. The other scaffolders also recounted what they had heard the three men talking about.
The wives of the Welshman and the Italian cried out in pain, "If only we'd known, we'd have changed the food."

But the wife of the Irishman looked puzzled. "But I don't understand," she said. "My husband always packed his own lunchbox."

* * *

Women are more irritable than men, probably because men are more irritating.

* * *

Three men were out mountain climbing when they discovered a cave in the side of the rock face.
"Cool! Let's go and explore," said one of them.
So in they went and stumbled across an old lamp.
"Hey, look at this. Wouldn't if be funny if it was a magic lamp!"
The others laughed but suddenly stopped in amazement as the man who had first spoken, rubbed the side of the lamp and out of the spout a genie materialised.
"I am the genie of the lamp and I will grant you one wish each."
"Great," said the first man. "Can you make me twice as clever as I already am?"
"Of course," replied the genie, and immediately the man began to quote great chunks out of Encyclopaedia Britannica.
The second man was so impressed, he asked to have his intelligence increased four times. Whoosh! the next minute the man was chalking fantastic mathematical equations all over the cave wall.
Then the third man spoke:
"This is incredible. Can you make me ten times as intelligent?"
"Are you sure you want that?" replied the genie. "It might be a bit alarming for you."
"Yes, yes, I'm sure," replied the man impatiently.
So the genie granted his wish and the man was turned into a woman.

* * *

Why do men like blonde jokes?
They can understand them.

* * *

Two men are walking through the jungle, one carrying a garden shed and the other a lump of concrete.
"What are you carrying that shed for?" asked the second man.
"Well if any dangerous animals come along, I can hide in the shed and remain unharmed," he said. "So why are you carrying a block of concrete?"
The second man gave him a knowing wink and replied, "If we meet any man-eating animals, I can throw down the concrete and make a faster getaway."

* * *

When a man says "I've got my reasons", he actually means, "I'll think of something in a minute."

* * *

Why do men drive BMW's?
Because they can spell the name.

* * *

Did you hear about the stupid man who went to the ironmonger's to get some screws?
"How long do you want them?" asked the shopkeeper.
"Well, actually, I was hoping to keep them," he replied.

* * *

A young man was riding a bicycle through town when he stopped to speak to his mate.
"Hello, Shaun, I didn't know you had a bicycle?"
"Yeah, I got it this morning when I was walking to work," replied

Shaun. "This beautiful girl rode up to me, got off her bicycle and then stripped off until she was completely naked."
"Get away!"
"Really! She then said I could have anything I wanted, so I chose the bicycle."
"Yeah, you did right," replied his friend. "The clothes would never have fitted you."

* * *

Did you hear about the stupid man who wanted to impress his girlfriend? He took her out to dinner and ordered everything in French. She was surprised, and so was the waiter. It was an Indian restaurant.

* * *

"My wife looks after me so well," said the simple man to his mate. "Last night I came home early to find a pair of trousers on the bedstead. She said she'd felt like buying me a present."

* * *

A very dumb man fell overboard from a cruise ship and was washed up on a deserted island. The only inhabitant was a beautiful young girl. Immediately she administered to his needs - taking him to her shelter, feeding him and supplying him with whisky washed up previously. When he had fully recovered, she asked him if he would like to play around.
He looked at her in astonishment and replied, "I can't believe my luck. All this and you've got a set of golf clubs too!"

* * *

"Professor," asked John, "how long can a man live without a brain?"
"I don't know; how old are you?" she replied.

If a man said what he thought, he'd be speechless.

* * *

A man stayed out very late drinking, staggered home and crept quietly into bed so he wouldn't wake his wife. Just as it started to get light, he woke up dying for a pee.
"Hey, Betty, there's three pairs of feet in our bed," he said nudging her.
"You daft oaf," she replied scornfully. "You can't see properly with all that booze in you. Get out and count again."
So the man went to the bottom of the bed and counted again.
"Sorry, you're right," he said. "There's only two pairs here and I can see I need my toenails cut."

* * *

Women don't make fools out of men. They only conduct the performance.

* * *

If ignorance is bliss, why aren't there more happy men?

* * *

A policeman was walking through Soho when he spotted a man kicking another man up the backside.
"Now, now, what's going on here?" he asked.
The first man explained, "It all goes back to when I was young. I met this beautiful girl and she invited me back to her place. When we got there, she took off her dress and then later she took off the rest of her clothes. So, of course, I turned down the heating and left. But it was then, as I was closing the door, that she told me one day I would realise what I had done and be so angry that I would ask the first man I saw to kick me up the backside. Well now I understand and I've asked this man to do just that."
"Right oh," said the policeman. "Carry on as you were."

Three women were out horse riding when they came across a magic lamp. On rubbing the lamp, a genie appeared who offered to make them more clever.
"Oh my!" exclaimed the first woman. "I'd like to be twice as clever as I am now", and immediately the genie turned her into a world-renowned doctor.
The second woman wished she could be three times as intelligent and she became a top nuclear scientist.
But the third woman, who was a model, was not interested.
"I get a lot of attention already," she replied, "and the more dumb I act, the more attention I get. So really I'd like to be a hundred times less intelligent."
And she got her wish. The genie turned her into a man.

* * *

Did you hear about the dumb man who invented an inflatable dartboard for campers?

* * *

How do you keep a man busy?
Put him in a round room and tell him to see in the corner.

* * *

"Just remember this!" shouted the angry man, "No woman ever made a fool out of me."
"Oh? Who did then?" she calmly replied.

* * *

A young girl went out with a boy who was very naive about lovemaking. When the girl discovered that he didn't know how to use a condom, she demonstrated by putting one on her thumb. Satisfied he

understood, they climbed into bed, switched off the light and began their lovemaking. However, after a while, the girl realised something was terribly wrong.
"John," she whispered, "I think the condom must have broken."
"Oh, no," he said, switching the light back on. "Look, here it is, quite safe on my thumb."

* * *

What's the similarity between a stupid man and an intelligent man? They both think they know everything.

* * *

What is a man doing when he holds his hands tightly over his ears? Holding onto a thought.

* * *

A husband comes home from work to find his wife in bed with another man. He goes absolutely berserk, ranting and raving for a good few minutes. Then he rushes to the wardrobe, pulls out his rifle and sticks the barrel in his mouth.
His wife jumps up screaming, "Bob! Don't, please."
"Shut up, you bitch!" he bellows. "You're next."

* * *

Did you hear about the stupid man who divorced his wife?
He was in the maternity unit waiting for her to deliver their baby when out came the midwife to tell him he had a beautiful set of twins.
The man put his head in his hands in anguish.
"Oh, no, I never thought she'd be unfaithful to me. Our marriage is over."
"But why?" asked the midwife. "There's nothing wrong here."
"Oh, but there is," he persisted. "We only did it once so the other one isn't mine."

A man walks into a take-away and orders a cheese and tomato pizza. When it arrives, the owner asks, "Shall I cut it into four pieces or eight?"
The man thinks for a moment and replies, "I'm feeling very hungry, cut it into eight pieces, please."

***

What's the similarity between dumb men and herpes?
You can't get rid of either, once you've got them.

***

A world-renowned professor invented a new lie detector which not only recognised when somebody told a lie, but also kicked the offender across the room.
He spent a day testing it out on people. First through the door came a young woman who was asked what qualifications she had. She told the professor she had a first class honours degree and immediately the machine kicked her across the floor. Then an older woman of 50 years came in and when she was asked her age, she replied 31. Again the machine kicked her across the room.
"Next, please," called the professor.
This time it was a young man.
"Why don't you give me your opinion on the way you view your life?" asked the professor.
"I think..." replied the man, but before he could say any more, he was kicked across the room.

***

A young couple were driving down a narrow country lane when suddenly the man took a corner too quickly and ploughed into the back of a car that had pulled up into the ditch to mend a puncture.
Badly shaken, the couple got out to inspect the damage but the driver

of the other car was nowhere to be seen. Then 100 yards down the road, they spotted a very small man sitting cross-legged on the ground, chanting to himself.
"Excuse me," said the man, "would you happen to know where the driver of this car has gone?"
"He has gone to get help," replied the little man, "but don't go. I must thank you for setting me free. I am a genie and I was imprisoned in that car for many years but now the crash has released me, so I can grant three wishes. One for each of you and the third for me."
Immediately the man said, "I wish for a Lotus Elan, what a beautiful car!"
"Then it will be yours," replied the genie.
"And I would like a house on millionaires' row," enthused the wife.
"Then, that too, will be yours." He continued, "Now it is my turn. I would like to have my way with your wife. It is many years since I had a woman."
Appalled at the idea, but realising their wishes would not come true if they refused, the wife and genie got into the back seat of the car and down to business.
Some minutes later, the genie sat back with a satisfied smile on his face and said, "By the way, how old is your husband?"
"Thirty-three," she replied, looking puzzled.
"Fancy that! Thirty-three and he still believes in genies!"

* * *

A man took his cat to the vet's because it seemed to be acting in a strange way.
"It looks to me as if she's going to have kittens," explained the vet. "I'll just do a few tests to make sure."
"But that's impossible," spluttered the man. "We live in a flat, 24 floors up, and she never goes out."
"So what you're saying is that she never comes into contact with any other cats?"
"Absolutely," confirmed the man. "But she's not lonely because we have a tom cat as well."

"But I don't understand," puzzled the vet...
The man interrupted "For goodness sake! it's not him, that's her brother."

* * *

A man came home and caught his wife in bed with another man.
"Hey!" he shouted, "what's going on here?"
The wife retorted, "See what I mean? I told you he was stupid."

* * *

An alien came down to earth and sought out a scientist that would allow him to take some brains back to his own planet for research purposes.
"This is an ape's brain," said the scientist. "It will cost you £250."
"Very good," replied the alien. "Have you anything else?"
"Yes, this is a woman's brain and it will cost £1,000."
"OK that's fine. And just one more possibly?"
"Well, this here, is a man's brain but it will cost you £5,000."
"Goodness me! Why is it so expensive?" the alien exclaimed.
"Well, it's hardly been used," replied the scientist.

* * *

"A man was asked by his boss to start up another office on the other side of the country. It would mean he'd be away from home for three weeks, so he called up his friend and asked him for a favour.
"Hello Matt, I'm going to be out of town on business for a while and I wonder if you'll secretly keep an eye on my wife while I'm gone. I just have these doubts that she's up to no good."
His friend agreed and after three weeks had passed, they met up again in the local pub.
"So what happened?" asked the husband.
"Sorry mate, not so good," replied Matt. "After a couple of days, a man appeared at the door, they kissed passionately and then went inside. It

was getting dark by this time and as the light in the kitchen was on, I could see them fondling each other frantically. Then the light went out and I saw them go up to your bedroom."
"What happened?" said the husband in despair.
"He stripped off, then undressed your wife and just at that moment, he came over and closed the curtains, so I couldn't see any more."
"Oh, no!" moaned the husband with his head in his hands. "You see what I mean? There is always the doubt."

* * *

Jake was a real wally. When he walked into the pub on Saturday morning, all the regulars burst into laughter.
"Hey, Jake, my old stud, we didn't know you had it in you," they laughed.
"What do you mean?" he replied.
"You wally. Last night, upstairs in your bedroom. You left the curtains open and you and your wife put on a great show for us all."
"Well, you lot are the wallies, not me," he replied with spirit. "I wasn't even at home last night."

* * *

What did the stupid man say to his unmarried pregnant daughter?
Don't worry, maybe it's not yours.

* * *

A pregnant woman is involved in a serious car crash and ends up in a coma for three months. When she finally awakes, the hospital tell her that they delivered her twins a few weeks earlier and both are doing well. She asks them where they are and is told that her uncle is looking after them and has had them christened.
"Oh, no!" she wails, knowing her uncle is a bit of an idiot. "What has he called them?"

The doctor replies, "He's called the little girl Denise."
"Oh, that's nice," she says thankfully, "and what has he called the boy?"
"De nephew."

* * *

Two simple-minded men, deciding to spend a night on the town, were discussing where they should go.
"I've heard of this great pub down the bottom of Market Street," enthused one of the men. "You get free drinks all night and then they take you out the back for some sex."
"Are you sure about that?" asked the other. "Sounds too good to be true."
"Oh, no, I promise you it's right, my sister goes there a lot and she told me."

* * *

A rather stupid man is driving along in his car when it gets involved in an accident with a lorry carrying nuts and bolts. The lorry sheds its load all over the car and damages it with lots of little dents.
So the next morning, the man takes it to the garage and explains to the mechanic what has happened.
Now the mechanic is an awful practical joker and once he realises the man is a right 'Herbert', he decides to have some fun. He tells the man to take the car home, blow up the exhaust pipe as hard as he can, and all the dents will pop out.
So the man does as he's told but no matter how hard he blows, the dents remain. Just then his flat mate, another 'Herbert', comes home from work and asks what is going on. After hearing the explanation, he looks at his friend and replies scornfully, "You great dumbo, of course it won't work, you need to roll the windows up first!"

* * *

What's the difference between a man and a supermarket trolley?
A supermarket trolley has a mind of its own.

* * *

Two simple men were walking through the woods when they stumbled across an old mirror. The first one picked it up, looked in it and said, "Hey, I know that bloke."
The second one took it from him and looked in it.
"Of course you do, you daft prat, it's me."

* * *

Big Jake was always being teased by his team mates about his sex life. "How's it going, Jake?" they asked him one day. "We hear you've been trying out a lot of new sexual positions."
"Yeah, that's true," said the big man proudly. "I'm just about ready to try them out on girls now."

* * *

Did you hear about the stupid man who started work on a building site?
After the first day, the boss came to congratulate him on his hard work. When he'd gone, the man turned to his fellow workmates and winked.
"I've really tricked the boss. I've been carrying the same load of bricks up and down the ladder all day."

* * *

A policeman came upon a stupid man peeing in the river.
"Stop that immediately!" he shouted, "And put it away."
So the stupid man did as he was told, but he couldn't stop himself from doubling up with laughter.

"OK, what's so funny?" demanded the policeman.
"I really fooled you this time," he laughed. "I may have put it away, but I didn't stop."

* * *

"Is that a gun in your pocket or are you just pleased to see me?"
"No, it's a gun."

* * *

One mother-in-law said to the other:
"I would never make a fool of my son-in-law. I've always allowed him to do that for himself."

* * *

Having just got married, the naive man said to his friend:
"Cor...was my girl dumb! She put the pillow under her bum instead of her head."

* * *

Why wasn't the man worried when his car was stolen?
He had the licence plate number.

* * *

If there is anything a man does not know, he imagines it.

* * *

The old building had fallen into such disrepair that a demolition gang moved in to raze it to the ground. Eventually, only the cellar was left and as they entered the one remaining room, they were horrified to see a skeleton in the corner. All that was left were the bones and a bright green sash, which read: 'Irish Hide And Seek Championship Finals 1949'".

* * *

What should you give a man who has everything?
A woman to show him how to work it.

* * *

"Mr Peterson, I have listened very carefully to your case," said the divorce judge, "and I have decided to award your wife £450 a month."
"Well, thank you very much, Your Honour, that seems very generous," replied Mr Peterson. "I'll try and throw a couple of quid in myself each month."

* * *

The wife turned to her husband and said, "It says here in this article that over 2,000 camels are used each year to make paint brushes."
"Really!" exclaimed her husband. "It's amazing what they can teach animals these days."

* * *

A "right Herbert" of a husband was so fed up with his wife telling him he was useless that he decided to give her a surprise. He decided to paint the bedroom. Early the next morning, after she had gone to work, he bought some paint and got down to work.
His wife returned home that evening and immediately smelled the new paint.
"Now what?" she thought. Up the stairs she went and into the bedroom to find her husband lying on the floor in a pool of sweat.
"Are you all right?" she asked, going up to him. "What are you doing?"

He gasped, "I just wanted to show you I'm not as useless as you think, so I decided to paint the bedroom."
She looked around and commented, "Well, it's very nice but why are you wearing your winter coat and your raincoat?"
"Well, it said on the directions 'for best results, put on two coats'."

* * *

My husband is so stupid, when he went to the mind reader, they gave him his money back.

* * *

He was so stupid, when he heard that 89 per cent of all crimes occur in the home, he moved.

* * *

A man arrives home early from work and hears strange noises coming from the bedroom. He rushes upstairs to discover his wife lying naked on the bed, sweating and panting heavily.
"What's going on?" he asks.
"I think I'm having a heart attack," she cries.
"Oh, no!" he gasps, but as he rushes back down the stairs to ring for an ambulance, he bumps into his five-year-old son.
"Daddy, daddy!" says the little boy excitedly. "Uncle Ted's upstairs in the wardrobe and he's got no clothes on."
"What!" roars the man and storms back up the stairs to the bedroom. He opens the wardrobe door and sure enough, Uncle Ted is standing there naked.
"You bastard, you bloody prat!" he screams. "How could you? There's my wife on the bed having a heart attack and all you can do is run around naked, playing hide and seek with the kids."

* * *

The man was so stupid, he sold his car for petrol money.

* * *

Giles had been shipwrecked on the desert island for more than two years and was missing female company badly. His only companions were a dog and a pig. The time came when the pig looked more and more attractive and one night, he decided to make his move. However, as he started to make his way over to the pig, he was attacked by the dog and stopped from going anywhere near it. Time after time he tried, but the ever-watchful dog would immediately start to growl, so he had to abandon his plans.

Then one day a beautiful young girl was washed up on the beach. The man took her to his shelter and nursed her back to health.

"You saved my life," she said with great feeling. "If there's anything you want in return, you only have to ask."

The man smiled broadly and replied "Oh wow! Great! Thanks a lot."

"Well, what would you like?" she whispered coyly.

"I wonder if you could take the dog for a walk," he replied.

* * *

It's a well known fact that you will often see clever men with thick women but very rarely see clever women with thick men.

* * *

MEN AT SPORT

Ben walked into the bar, heavily bandaged round the head, a black eye and a broken arm.
"Bloody hell!" exclaimed his mates. "What happened to you?"
"Playing golf is a dangerous game," he replied sorrowfully. "I was out on the 10th fairway with my wife, when she sliced the ball and it went sailing into a nearby field. It took us ages to find the ball and just as we were about to give up, I noticed it had lodged itself under a cow's tail. I went over and lifted the tail and called my wife over. All I said was, 'Sweetheart, this looks like yours' and wham!"

* * *

What do a man and a footballer have in common?
They both dribble when they're trying to score.

* * *

Why do men require instant replays on TV sports?
Because after 30 seconds, they forget what happens.

* * *

A woman rings the local cricket club asking to speak to her husband.
"I'm sorry madam," came the reply, "he's just gone out to bat."
"Oh, that's all right, I'll hold."

* * *

A man was sitting morosely over his pint of beer.
"What's wrong, Terry?" asked the landlord.
"It's the wife," he replied. "She's just run off with my best mate."
"The bastard!" exclaimed the landlord. "That's a dreadful thing to do."
"You're not wrong there, he was my partner in the final of the darts doubles championships tonight. Now we'll be disqualified!"

* * *

There may be many criticisms thrown at the English cricket team but women like them because they stay on top for two days but come second in the end.

* * *

The Lady Dowager was showing the Archbishop her race horses when one of them gave the most almighty fart.
"Oh my goodness," said the Lady Dowager, "how awful, I'm so terribly sorry."
"Not to worry," replied the Archbishop and then he added, "Actually, I thought it was the horse."

* * *

The football team was so bad, it had let in more goals than the rest of the division put together. After one really disastrous game, the manager told the players to gather round..
"Right lads, let's start at the beginning," he said sarcastically. "I have, here in my hand, a football, and the object of the game is to get this football..."
Suddenly he was interrupted by one of the players.
"Hold on, boss, you're going too fast."

* * *

The local football team were in the dressing room changing for their important local derby.
"Where's Tony?" asked the captain.
"He's getting married today at 2.30," came a voice from the back.
"Oh, damn!" cursed the goalkeeper. "That means he won't get here till the second half."

* * *

The husband had agreed to show his wife how to play golf. They walked up on to the first fairway and he told her to tee off. Lo and behold, she shot a hole in one. Then her husband walked up and said, "Not bad. Now I'll have my practice shot and then we'll start the game."

* * *

Bob was on his way out of the house to play golf, having just had an awful argument with his wife because she had wanted to go shopping. "It's quite true that I love golf more than I love you!" he yelled, but then, realising he'd overstepped the mark a bit, he continued in a softer voice, "But you know, I love you more than football."

* * *

Mabel had been out playing golf all morning when she received a message from the club house.
"Oh dear!" she exclaimed and ran onto the 17th fairway and up to a group of golfers.
"Excuse me," she said breathlessly, "would you mind if I played through? I've just heard my husband has been rushed to hospital with a heart attack."

* * *

A young couple decided to get married just four weeks after meeting at a night club.
"I know we don't know a lot about each other yet, but it'll just make our marriage more exciting as we find out," said the man. "Although I ought to mention that I love golf. I think about golf more than anything else."
"That's all right," said the woman, smiling. "It's good to be honest with each other. I think I ought to tell you that I'm a hooker."
The man took her in his arms and kissed her passionately. "You mustn't worry about that," he said gently. "There's probably a very easy explanation; no doubt you're putting your hands too far down the club."

* * *

A couple were out playing golf when suddenly a ball went hurtling past them, narrowly missing the man's head. A moment later, a woman appeared looking very flustered.
"I'm so sorry," she said, "are you all right?"
"No thanks to you," retorted the wife. "Why didn't you shout fore? You nearly hit my poor husband."
"Oh dear!" she exclaimed, and held out her club to the angry wife. "Here, feel free to take a shot at mine."

* * *

The manager of the local football club stormed into the changing room at half time and gave his team a severe dressing down.
"Right, you lily-livered, useless imbeciles, you bloody half-wits. Get out on that pitch immediately."
Everyone rushed out except one player sitting in the corner.
"Well?" shouted the manager, glaring at him.
"Well," responded the player, "there were certainly a lot of them, weren't there?"

* * *

MEN AT THE BAR

What's the difference between men and pigs?
Pigs don't turn into men when they get drunk.

* * *

"Did you know drinking makes you handsome?" said Val to her husband.
"Does it? But I don't drink," he said.
"I know, but I do!"

* * *

A man walked into a bar and exclaimed, "The drinks are on me, landlord, I'm celebrating."
"Congratulations," replied the landlord. "What's happened?"
"My wife and my best friend have gone away together," he said, smiling happily.
The landlord frowned, "I don't understand, doesn't that make you angry?"
"No way," he replied. "It has saved me a stack of money. They were both pregnant."

* * *

The devil walks into a pub and on seeing him, everyone, except for one woman at the bar, rushes out of the door as fast as possible. The devil walks up to the woman and says, "Don't you know who I am?"
"Of course I do," she says, turning away to have another drink.
Confused, the devil persists, "Well, aren't you scared of me?"
She replies, "I've been married to Bill for 30 years, I already know what hell is like."

A man with no arms went into a bar and ordered a pint of beer. When it arrived he asked the barman if he would reach over and get the money out of his jacket pocket. The barman obliged. Then the man asked him if he would hold the beer up to his lips so that he could drink it. The barman obliged.
"It must be quite difficult not having any arms," remarked the barman.
The man nodded, "Yes it is, and quite embarrassing sometimes. By the way, could you tell me where the gents is, please?"
After a moment's hesitation, the barman replied, "Sure mate, a couple of miles down the road, on your left."

* * *

A man was sitting at the bar crying into his beer when another bloke approached him.
"Hey, mate," he slurred, "what's up with you?"
"I'm drunk...again, and I've puked all over myself. I promised the wife I wouldn't and now she's sure to leave me," he wailed.
"No problem," replied his new friend. "Do as I do. Put a £10 note in your top pocket and when you get home, explain to the wife that some jerk puked all over you. Then show her the £10 note and tell her he gave it to you to get your clothes cleaned. It's easy."
"Yeah, that's great," said the first man, so he followed the plan closely and when he got home, faced up to his wife full of confidence. But when she saw him she went berserk. Ranting and raving, she told him she was off to pack her bags.
"Now hold on, darling," he said, swaying backwards and forwards. "Some drunk puked all over me. Look. He gave me £10 to get my clothes cleaned."
"Wait a minute," she said, "I thought you said he gave you £10; this is a £20 note."
"Yes, I know," agreed the man, "but he crapped in my pants as well."

* * *

A worried man walked into a pub and beckoned over the landlord.
"Do you remember me?" he asked. "Was I in here last night?"
"Yes, you were," replied the landlord.
"And did I spend a lot of money?"
"Oh, about £75," was the reply.
"Thank goodness for that," said the man, looking relieved, "I thought I'd wasted it."

* * *

"Good evening, madam, I'm collecting for the new home for alcoholics. Can you donate anything?"
"Come back a bit later," she replied. "You can have my husband after closing time."

* * *

A woman walks into a bar and orders a gin and tonic. She finishes it off in two minutes and orders a refill. Having gulped that down, she looks in her handbag and then orders a third drink. Once that's finished, she looks in her handbag again and calls for another.
By this time the landlord is so curious, he has to ask her why she keeps looking in her handbag before ordering a drink. The woman looks at him for a moment, swaying from side to side, and answers, "I have a picture of my husband in this bag and when he starts to look good, then I go home."

* * *

A man stopped off for a quick drink on the way home but one drink led to many and by the time it was 11 o'clock he was as drunk as a skunk. He staggered home, crept up the garden path but tripped over a rake that had been left lying about and landed on the up-turned spikes, damaging his backside quite considerably.
However, he was determined not to wake the wife, so he went as

quietly as he could into the bathroom, checked his backside in the mirror and repaired it as well as he could with sticking plasters. The following morning he woke up with a throbbing headache, and if that wasn't enough, he had to face the wife.
"You were blind drunk last night," she accused him.
"No I wasn't," he said lamely, "I only had a couple."
"Rubbish!" she replied. "You must have been legless."
"Why? What makes you say that?" he asked.
"When I got up this morning," she said grimly, "there was a pile of plasters stuck on the mirror!"

* * *

One evening a man comes home in a terrible temper.
"What's wrong with you?" asks the wife.
"It's that bloody smarmy landlord at the Kings Head. He reckons he's slept with every woman on this street except one."
She thinks for a minute and then replies, "It'll be her at number eight, stuck up cow."

* * *

"James Ronald Simpkins, you are up before the bench today because of alcohol," said the judge. "Alcohol has caused you to be in this present predicament."
The man replied, "Oh your honour, thank you very much. Everyone else said it was my fault."

* * *

It was a big event. People from far and wide were arriving at the Pig and Whistle to watch the strongest man in the county competition. Many men had fallen by the wayside until just one remained. A huge grizzly specimen, 6'6" tall, weighing over 20 stone. His last feat was to squeeze every drop of juice out of an orange and defy anyone to beat him.

"There," he roared, "not a drop left. Anyone dare contradict me?"
Suddenly there was movement at the back of the crowd and a little man walked forward. He was only 5'6" tall and couldn't have weighed more than nine stone. The pub erupted into laughter as the little man said timidly, "Excuse me. I can do better than that."
The next moment he had taken the orange off the big man, squeezed out another two drops and was proclaimed the strongest man in the county.
Afterwards the big man took the new champion aside.
"Hey, mate, what do you do for a living, a weightlifter or what?"
"No, no," said the little man, "I'm a tax inspector."

* * *

A group of men were chatting in the bar when suddenly a stunning redhead walked in. The men stopped talking and whistled at her as she came up to them.
"Hello lads, don't you recognise me? It's me, Frank. I'm Frankie now, since the sex change operation."
The men were astounded but very curious to know all the details.
"Hey, Frankie, what was the most painful part of the operation? Was it having your dick cut off?"
"Oh no," he/she replied.
"Well, was it when you had your balls lopped off?"
"No, no," Frankie replied, "the most painful part was when they opened up my head and increased my brain."

* * *

A bloke walks into a pub with a pot-bellied pig on a lead.
"Bloody hell," said the barman, "that's got to be one of the ugliest animals I've ever seen."
"Yeah," replied the pig, "I picked him up at the market last week."

* * *

A drunk staggered into the police station to complain about his car. "Someone's been in my car," he slurred, "and taken the steering wheel, the brake, the pedals, the dashboard, bloody everything!" Seeing the man was so drunk, the duty officer humoured him for a few moments and said he'd come and investigate after he'd made an urgent phone call. So the drunk staggered back outside, but returned again five minutes later.
"Don't bother, officer," he said. "It's all right now. It was my mistake; I got into the back seat."

* * *

A man staggered out of the pub, having spent all day drinking, and fell headlong into a deep trench. A passer-by rushed up to him and said, "Hey, what happened?"
"I don't know," replied the drunk. "I only just got here myself."

* * *

The phone rang and the barman went to answer it. After listening for a moment, he replied:
"I'm sorry madam, you'll have to give me a better description, this place is full of no-good layabouts who should be at home."

* * *

"Good afternoon, Landlord, a pint of less, if you please," said the old man.
"Less? Never heard of it," replied the barman.
"Oh, come now, surely you have," he persisted.
"No, sorry, we certainly don't stock it. What is it anyway? Some foreign beer?"
"Well, I'm not sure," admitted the man. "It was my doctor who mentioned it. He said I should drink less."

* * *

A man walked into a pub and saw a huge Great Dane standing by a bloke at the bar.
"Does your dog bite?" he asked.
"No, never," replied the man. "He's as gentle as a lamb."
So the newcomer put out his hand to stroke the dog and nearly got it bit off.
"Hey! I thought you said your dog was gentle," he said angrily.
"It is," replied the man, "but this isn't my dog."

* * *

Two stupid men (so what's new?) meet in the bar and one says to the other.
"Hey! can you tell me what the date is, please?"
"No idea," says the other.
"But you've got a newspaper in your pocket," he says.
"Sorry mate, it's no use, it's yesterday's."

* * *

My husband always drinks with a friend. That way he's got someone to carry him home.

* * *

The landlord approached the man at the end of the bar and said, "Excuse me, Fred, I can't help notice that when you have a drink, you shut your eyes."
"Doctor's orders," replied the man. "He told me never to look at a pint again."

* * *

A drunk walked into a bar crying his eyes out.
"What's happened?" said one of his mates, looking very concerned.
"I've just done a dreadful thing!" sobbed the drunk. "This morning I sold my wife for a bottle of whisky."

"Oh, no, that really is awful," agreed his mate, "and I suppose you want her back now?"
"I do, I do," he sniffed.
"And I guess you realise now that you truly love her," he continued.
"Oh, no," replied the drunk. "I want her back because I'm thirsty again."

* * *

MEN AT THE BUTT END

Just think girls!
When you've adam
Don't they make you eve.

* * *

What's the similarity between men and toilets?
They're either vacant, engaged or full of shit.

* * *

A young girl, working as an au pair abroad, is distraught to receive a letter from her boyfriend breaking off their engagement and asking for his photograph back. So she spends the next few days gathering up as many pictures of men as she can find and sends them all back to him with a little note saying, "Can't remember which one you are, so please take out your photo and return the rest to me."

* * *

Boys will be boys, but one day all girls will be women.

* * *

A man went to the doctor's covered in bruises, lacerations and suffering from a broken arm.
"Good gracious, man, what happened to you?" asked the doctor.
"My wife had another nightmare," he replied.
"Come off it! She couldn't have inflicted all these injuries!" exclaimed the doctor.

"Oh, she didn't, doctor. But you see, when she had the nightmare, she shouted out, 'Quick get out of here, my husband's coming home' and naturally in my dazed state, I jumped out of the window!"

* * *

The woman went round to her friend's house for tea.
"I have to tell you, Julie, my husband's a real bastard. He does nothing but find fault with everything I do, yet I know he's bedding his bloody secretary. It's driving me to distraction. I can't sleep, I can't eat. Do you know, I've lost half a stone these last couple of weeks."
"Well, get rid of the jerk, Patsy, and take him for everything he's got," urged her friend.
"Oh, I'm going to, don't worry. But first I want to lose another stone."

* * *

The more men I meet, the more I like my dog.

* * *

A man came home unexpected and discovered his wife in bed with the lodger.
"Hey, you bastard!" he shouted, "is this the way to thank us for our hospitality in taking you off the streets... and stop doing that while I'm talking to you."

* * *

One woman to another.
"How do you keep your youth?"
"Lock him up in the wardrobe, of course."

* * *

A man had been away for a week on business, but finished quicker than first planned, so he sent a telegram to his wife telling her he'd be home the next day and was bringing a friend with him. Alas, the following evening, he walked into the bedroom to find his wife in the throes of passion with another man. The husband went absolutely berserk, threatening to beat the living daylights out of them both, there and then.
"Hold on, Mike, there must be some logical explanation. Just calm down and leave it to me," urged his friend.
Sure enough, the following day the friend, looking triumphant, told the husband that, yes, there was an explanation:
"It seems there was a postal strike on the day you sent the telegram, so she didn't receive it!"

* * *

Why is a man like a bad violin player?
They both sit there scratching away instead of learning to use their instruments properly.

* * *

What do you call a man who sits at your front door?
Matt.

* * *

The man turned to his girlfriend and said,
"Oh, Julie, why don't you let me know when you have an orgasm?"
"I would," she said, "but you're never there."

* * *

Old Martha, spinster of the parish, rang the police one evening to report she'd captured a burglar climbing in through her bedroom window. She asked them to pick him up the following morning!

A man is walking past an empty supermarket trolley when he hears a woman's voice behind him.
"Excuse me, do you want that trolley?"
"No," he replies, "I'm only after one thing."
"Typical man," she mutters as she walks away.

* * *

A thoroughly bad couple decided to smuggle some wild animals out of their native country and into Britain.
"It's easy," said the wife. "Just stick this skunk down the front of your trousers when you go through customs."
"But what about the smell?" protested the husband.
"Well...if it dies, it dies," she replied.

* * *

"It's a waste of time trying to change a man's character. You have to accept your husband as he is."
Queen Elizabeth II

* * *

Women have a great sense of humour. Take the average man, for instance: that's proof enough that women can take a joke.

* * *

What's the similarity between men and parking spaces?
The good ones always go first and the ones that are left are disabled.

* * *

What's the definition of a boring man?
Here today and here tomorrow.

The woman had been looking at the garden hoses for more than 10 minutes, so the garden centre manager went over to find out what the problem was.
"I can't decide whether to buy a hose with or without its stand," she said. "You see, it's a birthday present for my husband."
"Well, that'll be a nice surprise," he replied.
"Oh. it'll certainly be a surprise," she said with gusto. "He thinks he's getting a crate of whisky!"

* * *

Three people got into the lift - the perfect man, the perfect woman and Superman. Looking down, they saw a £50 note on the floor. Who do you think picked it up?
It was the perfect woman, of course. The other two don't exist.

* * *

Relaxing after Sunday lunch, Bob turned to his wife and said,
"Maisie, if I die before you, do you think you'll get married again?"
"Maybe," she replied.
"And would you both go to the places we go together now, like the social club and the Horse and Hounds?" he persisted.
"Probably," she replied.
"But you wouldn't give him my championship darts, would you?"
"Of course not," she replied. "He uses a different weight."

* * *

A group of nuns were attending a lecture on how to look after themselves. The speaker turned to one of the nuns and asked her what she would do if she were accosted by a man.
"I would lift up my habit and tell the man to drop his trousers."
"Goodness me!" replied the speaker, looking shocked. "And then what?"

"I would run away as fast as I could, and I can run much faster with my habit up than he can run with his trousers down."

* * *

What do you give a man who has everything?
Penicillin.

* * *

Two nurses were climbing through a window into the nurses' home after a night on the town.
"This makes me feel like a burglar," whispered one.
"And me," whispered the other. "But where would we get a burglar at this time of night?"

* * *

Two women talking on the top deck of a bus.
"Anyhow, my dream come true would be to have two men at once."
"Really?"
"Oh yes, one in the kitchen cooking, and the other doing the cleaning."

* * *

Women are called birds because of all the worms they pick up.

* * *

How does a man cook dinner?
I don't know, he never has.

* * *

What's the difference between a hedgehog and a man who drives a Porsche?
With a hedgehog, the prick is on the outside.

A man rushed into the chemist's and asked the woman behind the counter if she had anything for a permanent erection.
"One moment," she said. "I'll just go and ask my sister."
A few minutes later she returned smiling.
"After talking to my sister, we've decided a 25 per cent stake in the business and £1,000 in cash is our best offer!"

* * *

A man was urged by his mates to have his fortune read by Psychic Lil on the prom at Blackpool. Now the man was not a believer; in fact, he found the whole thing very stupid, but he crossed her palm with silver and she looked into the crystal ball.
"Ah ha!" she eventually said. "I see you are the father of three children."
"Well, you're wrong there," he smirked, "it's four children actually."
The fortune teller looked at him and smiled. "That's what you think," she said.

* * *

God must have been disappointed in Adam - He made Eve so different.

* * *

The stagecoach was held up by a band of armed desperados.
"Everyone out!" yelled the gang leader. "We're going to rob all the men and have our wicked way with all the women."
"Hey, boss," said his sidekick, "let's just rob the men and get out of here fast."
Hearing this, an old woman at the back shouted, "Now just wait a minute, who's in charge round here?"

* * *

What do men and greasy hair have in common?
They're both limp, lank and lifeless when you want a bit of body.

* * *

What's the difference between a man and a puppy?
Eventually a puppy will mature and stop whining.

* * *

A very obese man had been coming to the gym for more than a month, huffing and puffing on the exercise machines, looking thoroughly miserable.

One Friday night, however, he suddenly stood stock still on the running machine, looked very worried.

"What's up?" asked the instructor.

"I've just realised something," he said. "I've been coming to this gym because a few weeks ago my wife said she wanted to make mad passionate love to someone muscular and thin...and now I know what she meant."

* * *

Women like the simple things in life - like men.

* * *

She said, "That's a nice suit you have on. I wonder if it will ever come back into fashion."

* * *

Why are men and seagulls alike?
You should never look up to either of them.

He said, "I've got an idea."
"Beginner's luck," she replied.

* * *

A spry old lady, driving along in her Bentley, spotted a parking space on the busy high street. She drove past, ready to back in, when an arrogant young man in a sports car quickly drove in before her. "Sorry, madam," he said cheekily as he jumped out. "You've got to be young and zippy to do that."
The old lady said nothing. She just continued to back into the space that had been there. Very soon there was the sound of broken glass and crunching metal as the Bentley hit the front of the sports car before continuing to drive right over the top of it.
"There, young man," she said, stepping majestically out of her car. "You have to be old and rich to do that."

* * *

What would be your ideal man?
One who makes wonderful love for hours and then turns into an Indian take-away!

* * *

"Mummy, mummy!" cried the little boy. "In our lesson at school today, the teacher said I was descended from apes, gorillas and monkeys. Is that right?"
"I don't know, sweetheart," she replied. "I never knew any of your father's family."

* * *

How do you know if a man's going to be unfaithful?
He has a penis, hasn't he?

If you want your husband to listen, then talk to another man.

* * *

A vicar and a woman carrying a baby found themselves sitting next to each other on the 9.40am train from Paddington to Penzance. After leaving Reading, the vicar said to the woman:
"I must say, that's a gorgeous bonny little girl you have there; you must be very proud."
"Oh indeed I am," she replied, "and even more so because it took ten years of marriage before I conceived."
"Really? I've always said one must never give up; one must always follow one's dreams. Take me, for instance. I breed a very rare species of chicken and for more than a year things were not going as well as they might and the chickens seemed very dispirited. But now! Why, it's incredible. The chickens are breeding well and laying a record number of eggs."
"What made the difference?" she asked.
"Oh, I changed the cock," he replied.
"So did I," she said.

* * *

A woman went into the chemist's, and blushing profusely, asked for a packet of condoms. The assistant showed her a number of sizes but they were all too big. Eventually he got out a dwarf size packet but she still insisted they were far too big.
At this point, the assistant looked at her sympathetically and said, "Excuse me, madam, but it does seem as if your husband is rather poorly endowed."
"What!" she exclaimed. "How dare you! I want something for the mice problem we have!"

* * *

Every Thursday morning the women in the Close would meet for coffee and a chat.
For a few months this was a peaceful interlude in their busy lives until a new neighbour appeared who was rather coarse. She would always have something unsavoury to tell them, no matter how much they protested. So the group decided that the next time she started one of her stories, they would all walk out.
Sure enough, the following Thursday, just as coffee had been made, the new arrival began:
"Well, ladies, you'll never believe this. The local brothel has lost a few of its best girls recently, so they're holding interviews tomorrow morning for anyone who's interested."
At that, all the women stood up and marched out.
"Hey, wait a minute," said the new neighbour in surprise. "There's no need to rush; they're not interviewing until tomorrow morning!"

* * *

"New York City has finally hired women to pick up garbage, which makes sense to me, since, as I've discovered, a good bit of being a woman consists of picking up garbage."
Anna Quindlen

* * *

Overheard on the top deck of a bus:
"Chocolate's better than sex.
It's satisfying even when it's soft."

* * *

Two old ladies were talking over tea.
"But I thought you couldn't stand the man, Beryl; I'd never have dreamt you'd let him marry your daughter."
"You're quite right, Jane," replied Beryl, looking smug, "but just imagine the fun I'll have being his mother-in-law."

An international committee of women have officially announced that computers should be referred to as masculine.
They gave their reasons as follows:
a) In order to get their attention, you have to turn them on.
b) They may have a lot of data, but they are still clueless.
c) Instead of helping you solve problems, half the time they are the problem.
d) As soon as you make a commitment to one, you realise that if you'd waited a little longer, you could have had a better model.

* * *

My husband boasts that he is a self-made man. Well, at least that relieves God of an awful responsibility.

* * *

Why was alcohol invented?
So ugly men could have sex.

* * *

When God created the earth, he made Eve first, but He gave her three breasts. After a while Eve complained that her breasts were giving her a lot of trouble. They kept bumping into each other and causing pain. So God remedied the situation by getting rid of the middle breast.
A few weeks later, Eve complained to God again.
"I'm so bored," she said. "Would it be possible to have someone to play with?"
"That's a good idea," said God. "I'll call him man. Now where did I put that useless tit?"

* * *

Said the girl to the man who was pestering her,
"I bet they call you bedspread because you're always getting turned down!

* * *

How do you know when a man's about to say something smart?
He starts the sentence with "A woman once told me..."

* * *

Why do some men have clean consciences?
Because they're never used.

* * *

What would you do if you saw your ex writhing around the floor in agony?
Shoot him again.

* * *

Two women talking on the top deck of a bus.
"I've had it with men," said Rosie. "They lie, they cheat, they have no conscience. No more. From now on, when I want sex, I'll use a vibrator."
"But what if the batteries run down?" asked her friend. "What will you do then?"
"Just what I do with my boyfriend; I'll fake an orgasm."

* * *

What's the difference between a penis and a bonus?
Your wife will always blow a bonus.

The man couldn't believe it when he saw the card in the newsagent's window advertising a two-year-old Mercedes for sale at just £100. At first, he thought it must be a misprint but when he rang the number, the woman assured him that it was all above board and she wanted £100. Later that morning he went round to see the car, and there it was gleaming in the midday sun. The bodywork was perfect and the engine purred like a cat.
"But why is it so cheap?" he asked puzzled. "I have to say you could get a lot more for it."
"Maybe," she said, "but this is exactly what I want. Last month my husband ran off with his secretary and a couple of days ago he rang to ask me to sell his car and send him the money."

* * *

How can you tell when a man is well hung?
When you can't get your finger in between his neck and the noose.

* * *

Said the arrogant man, "I climb mountains for a hobby, but getting on top of you is probably going to be my biggest challenge to date."
She replied calmly, "Well, that depends on the length of your rope."

* * *

From the moment they were married Colin had been desperate to find out more about his wife's past romantic attachments.
"Oh, please, Tracy, how many men have you slept with? Please tell me, I won't be angry," he pleaded.
"Are you sure?" she asked doubtfully.
"I promise, cross my heart," he begged.
"Well...OK...let me think. One...two...three...four...you... six...seven..."

What does it mean when a man is in bed, gasping for breath and calling your name?
You didn't hold the pillow down long enough.

* * *

Two women talking over the garden wall.
"I think our new doctor's absolutely gorgeous," said one.
"I'm not so sure," said the other. "Take away his hair, his eyes, his lips and his smile, and what have you got?"
"I don't know."
"My husband," she sighed.

* * *

Why are babies slapped on the bottom when they are first born?
To knock all the penises off the brainy ones.

* * *

A poor long-suffering wife was saddled with one of the laziest husbands in Britain. All he did was lounge on the sofa, smoking fags and drinking beer, and constantly issuing orders to her.
One morning the tap in the bathroom started dripping and she tentatively asked her husband if he would mend it for her.
"Sod off!" he replied. "Do I look like a plumber?"
Later in the day, the lock on the back door broke and again she approached her husband.
"Sorry to bother you, luv, but will you have a look at the back door; the key's got stuck."
"Bugger off! Since when did I look like a locksmith? Now go and get me a cold beer."
Eventually the wife was able to get two men out to look at both the tap and the lock.

When she informed her husband that the repairs had been done, he asked her how much it cost.
"Well," she said, "they both said I could either pay by baking a cake or having sex."
"Oh, yeah, so what did you bake them?"
"Who do you think I am, Delia Smith?"

***

How can you tell if your husband is dead?
The sex is the same but at least you get the remote.

***

MEN AT THEIR WEAKEST

How many real men does it take to change a light bulb?
None. Real men aren't afraid of the dark.

* * *

The latest group of men from earth had arrived at the Pearly Gates and were waiting to enter. The men were supposed to be queuing behind one of two signs. The first read: 'Henpecked husbands here', and the queue went on for miles. The second sign read: 'Independent husbands here', and behind this stood one forlorn looking man. When the keeper of the gate saw this, he asked the man standing alone why he was standing behind the 'Independent husbands' sign.
"My wife told me to," he replied meekly.

* * *

What's the similarity between a weak wally and an old car?
They both need a great deal of touching up to get them going.

* * *

A cowboy rides into a rough frontier town and walks into the saloon.
"I'll have a shot of whiskey," he demands from the barman and downs it in one gulp. After another couple of drinks, which he takes more slowly, he leaves the saloon only to return seconds later shouting at the top of his voice:
"Whichever one of you damned critters stole my horse, if it's not

back by the time I've had another drink, I'll do what I did in Coyote Creek."
So the man has another drink and goes back outside to see his horse has been returned.
As he mounts to ride away, the barman comes rushing up to him.
"Hey, mister, just out of interest, what did you do in Coyote Creek?"
"I had to walk home," replies the man.

* * *

"Bob," whispered his wife urgently, "I think I can hear someone moving around downstairs. Are you awake?"
"No," he replied.

* * *

The man was so henpecked, he had to wash and iron his own apron.

* * *

What do men and rolls of carpet have in common?
Lay them properly the first time and you can walk all over them for the rest of their lives.

* * *

The man behind the bar said to Colin:
"You really are a typical example of a spineless, henpecked man."
"Now look here," replied Colin, "you wouldn't say that if my wife was here."

* * *

"Darling," said the husband, "what's your favourite sexual position?"
"Across the street," she replied.

The best way to get a man to do something is to suggest he's far too old to do it.

* * *

What is the smartest thing a man can say?
"My wife says..."

* * *

Women - what have you got when you have two little balls in your hand?
A man's undivided attention.

* * *

What's the difference between pink and purple?
The woman's grip.

* * *

An old woman is sitting quietly in her garden when suddenly a genie appears and grants her three wishes.
"I would like to be very rich and live in a mansion," she says.
Wooosh! Her house turns into a mansion and fantastic gold jewellery adorns her body.
"Secondly, I would like to be young and beautiful so I can enjoy my new found wealth."
Wooosh! And her wish is granted.
"Finally," she says seeing her trusty dog lying on the lawn, "I would like my dog to be turned into the most handsome man that ever walked the earth."
Wooosh! And there in front of her is the most perfect man. The woman can't believe her eyes.
"Oh, my, you're incredible," she whispers.
He replies, "Now don't you wish you'd never had me castrated."

A man who had pleaded not guilty beforehand was now in court watching the jury of nine women and two men take their seats. All of a sudden he turned to his barrister and whispered frantically in his ear.
"Your Honour," said the barrister rising, "my client would like to change his plea to guilty."
"And may I ask why he has changed his mind?" demanded the judge.
"Of course. When he pleaded not guilty he didn't realise there would be so many women on the jury. He tells me he can't fool one woman so there's no chance he'd fool nine of them."

* * *

"Is your husband easy to please?"
"I don't know, I've never tried."

* * *

"Well, isn't that a coincidence?" she said. "You look just like my fourth husband."
"Fourth!" he gasped. "How many have you had?"
"Three."

* * *

The man sat staring morosely into his pint of beer.
"What's wrong, mate?" asked the sympathetic barman. "Is it woman trouble?"
"Too right," replied the man. "I've just had an awful fight with my wife."
"What happened?"
"She came crawling over to me on her hands and knees..."
"Oh, no," interrupted the barman, "what happened next?"
"She said she'd put me in hospital for a week if I didn't get out from under the bed."

Women's Lib is making him sleep on the wet bit.

* * *

Behind every great woman there's a man who's disappointed her.

* * *

"Every man who is high up likes to feel that he has done it all himself; and the wife smiles, and lets it go at that. It's our only joke. Every woman knows that."
J M Barrie 'What Every Woman Knows'

* * *

Our dad thinks he wears the trousers in our house, but it's mum who tells him which pair to put on.

* * *

No man is really successful until his mother-in-law admits it.

* * *

The henpecked husband said he couldn't bear to sit through porno movies.
"Why not?" asked a mate.
"Because I can't stand to see one guy enjoying himself more in ten minutes than I have in twenty-five years."

* * *

A businessman is walking along the beach when he spots an old bottle washed up on the shore. When he opens it, a genie slowly emerges and whispers, "Hello, I am the genie of the bottle, but I'm not

so well, so I can only grant you one wish - and it'd better be an easy one."
"I wish for an end to the recession in this country."
"Oh, that's hard," replies the genie. "Can you give me something easier?"
"OK, can you make my mother-in-law respect me?"
The genie replies, "So you want an end to the recession, do you?"

* * *

Many a wife has helped her husband to the top rung of the ladder – and then left him there for a while until she's decided whether the picture would look better somewhere else.

* * *

The children were being asked questions in their Sunday School lesson.
"Now," said the teacher, "who is it that we all tremble before, bow our heads and declare our unworthiness?"
A little boy at the back put his hand up. "Please miss, it's my mum. Because that's what I see my dad do every Saturday night when he wants some beer money."

* * *

A wife and her henpecked husband are having dinner in a restaurant. The waiter comes over to take their order.
"I'll have the lamb steak with garlic butter," says the woman.
"And the vegetable, madam?" asks the waiter.
"Oh, he'll have the same as me."

* * *

Two men talking over a pint in the pub:
"My wife and I had an awful argument on Tuesday. She wanted to go to the opera and I wanted to go bowling. Anyway, we sorted it out in the end."
"Good. So what was the opera like?"

"Doctor, doctor, my wooden leg is giving me such a lot of pain."
"Don't be silly, man," replied the doctor. "How can a wooden leg give you pain?"
"My wife keeps hitting me on the head with it."

* * *

The President of the world's most successful international business, accompanied by his wife, stop for petrol at a small out-of-the-way garage. As the garage attendant comes out to help them, the wife looks up and screams with pleasure.
"John, oh, no! I can't believe it!" She jumps out of the car and rushes to embrace him. Then after a few minutes of animated conversation, she returns to the car looking very thoughtful.
As they drive off, the husband looks at her with interest and asks, "Who was that, sweetheart?"
"That was an old boyfriend of mine. We were together a long time. In fact, we almost got married."
There is a moment's silence and then he says, "Ah, well. I guess you're glad you married me instead."
"What makes you say that?"
"Because I'm the President of an international company."
"That's quite irrelevant," she replies with scorn. "If I'd married John, he would now be President."

* * *

How do men sort their laundry?
"Filthy" and "filthy but all right for another couple of days".

* * *

A beautiful young woman goes to see her psychiatrist because she keeps getting recurring nightmares. The psychiatrist asks her to lay down on the couch and the next moment he's on top of her and they make love. When it's over, he says:

"Right, that takes care of my problem. Now let's hear what your trouble is."

✻ ✻ ✻

"Doctor, doctor, can you come round and see my wife as soon as possible? She is so ill. I had to carry her downstairs to make my dinner."

✻ ✻ ✻

A married man went on business to London and met a beautiful young girl. They spent five idyllic days together and at the end of his stay, he bade her farewell and offered to leave her some money.
The girl shook her head. "No thanks, darling, you go back to your wife. I don't want anything, I'm a good sport."
Time went by and it was four months later that the man received a phone call from her.
"Oh, thank goodness I've found you," she sobbed. "I've discovered I'm pregnant. I can't believe it! I'm going to do away with myself."
"My goodness," replied the man admiringly, "you really are a good sport, aren't you."

✻ ✻ ✻

Two men were talking about their sons over a pint of beer.
"My son must be the laziest bugger in the world," complained Alan. "He never does a thing."
"No," argued Bob. "My son is the laziest."
After discussing this problem for a while, they decide to go to each other's houses to check it out. When they get to Alan's house, they find his son lying on the sofa, watching TV and surrounded by sweet papers.
"Hey, son, pop down the road and get me an evening paper."
"No chance," replied the boy.

"Go on, I'll give you a couple of quid for going."
"Leave me alone, go away," came the reply.
So the two men went over to Bob's house and discovered his son lying on the sofa, watching the TV, the fire full on, the boy dripping with sweat, but also crying."
"What's up, son?" asked his father.
It took a while for his son to answer but eventually he replied, "I can't change channels, dad, the remote's fallen off the back of the sofa."

***

The angry husband stormed into the pub and confronted a man, quietly drinking at the bar.
"You bastard!" shouted the husband. "Thought you could get away with it, did you? Well, think again. I've got proof right here that you've been carrying on with my wife."
He took some photographs out of his pocket and showed them to the man.
"See," he continued. "This is a picture of you and my wife drinking together in the pub. And this one shows you kissing her in the back of your car...and look at this, in this one she's half undressed. What have you got to say for yourself?"
The man studied each of the photos for a few minutes and then replied, "I'll take six copies of photo number three."

***

Why are men so quiet when they have sex?
They don't talk to strangers.

***

"My bloody stupid boyfriend is going to die of syphilis!" cried the distraught woman.
"Oh, no," replied her friend. "No one dies of syphilis anymore."
"Well they do, if they give it to me," she retorted.

A man returned from the doctor's with some very bad news. He had been told that his sex life was nearly over because he had simply worn out his tackle.
"I would estimate that you have about 30 sessions left," said the doctor sympathetically.
When the man told his wife she was shocked.
"Oh, no, how can this be? Only 30 left! We must make every one of these very special. Let's make a plan now."
"I have," he said. "I made a schedule on the way home and your name isn't on it."

* * *

A wife rang up her husband in anguish.
"Jack, Jack, the doctor says I'm pregnant. Why didn't you use a condom?"
"But I always use a condom," he argued. "Anyway, who is this?"

* * *

When a woman says...
"Come on Shaun, this place is a hovel. You and me need to clean it up. Put away everything lying on the bed, and then all the stuff on the floor ought to go into the washing machine immediately or we'll have no clothes left."
The man hears...
"Na na na you and me na na na on the bed na na na immediately na na na no clothes."

* * *

A despicable husband was travelling round the country buying new merchandise for his department store. His trip lasted much longer than usual, so he would keep in touch with his wife by sending her telegrams saying, "Still travelling, still buying".

After two more weeks had passed, the wife eventually sent a message back to him.
'Come home at once or I'll be selling what you're buying!'

* * *

"If I say no to going to bed with you, will you really commit suicide?"
"Well, that's my usual procedure, yes," he said.

* * *

Did you hear about the innocent young girl who met a man in a raincoat?
Later, she recounted the event to her friend.
"Coming back from the supermarket this morning, a man stopped me in the car park and showed me the lining of his raincoat."
"That's odd," mused her friend. "Are you sure he only wanted you to see his raincoat?"
"Oh yes, he wasn't wearing anything else."

* * *

When man was first made, he only had twenty years of normal sex life. To him, this was horrifying. Meanwhile, the monkey had also been given twenty years normal sex life but he said he only needed ten years, so he gave the other ten to the man.
Likewise, the lion, also with twenty years, gave ten years to the man as well. He agreed that ten years was plenty.
Finally the donkey, agreeing with the other animals that ten years was enough, gave the man another ten years.
So all this explains today's modern man. He has twenty years of normal sex life, ten years of monkeying around, a further ten years of lion about it and finally ten years of making a complete ass of himself.

"I'm leaving you!" screamed the man's wife. "You've messed around just once too often. I overheard that tart from number 38 tell her friends that you had a small penis. Oh the shame!"
"The truth is," replied the husband, "that she has a big mouth."

* * *

After their honeymoon, the husband brought his wife breakfast in bed. On the tray was fresh orange juice, cereal, bacon and egg, toast and coffee.
"Mmm, thank you darling," she said. "This looks lovely."
"Good," he replied, "because that's how I want it every morning."

* * *

The doctor received a call from one of the local farmers.
"If you have a moment, would you mind popping in to have a look at the wife, doctor?"
"Of course," replied the doctor. "Is she feeling unwell?"
"I'm not sure. This morning she got up, as usual, at 4.30, milked the cows, took the sheep up to the top field, cooked the breakfast for myself and the lads, prepared the books for the accountant, cleaned out the barn, made dinner, sorted the hens, went to market, got my supper, cleaned up and then organised events for next week's harvest festival. When she finished at midnight, she complained she felt a bit tired. Maybe she just needs a pick-me-up."

* * *

Two men shared a flat in Fulham. On Saturday night, one of them arrived home to find ten crates of beer, four bottles of scotch and a loaf of bread on the kitchen table.
"Hey, mate," he said. "You didn't tell me we were having a party?"
"We're not," replied the second man.
"Then what's the bread for?"

Said the wife to her lazy husband:
"Listen Bert, you're going to make yourself ill, sitting there all day thinking up excuses for not working."

* * *

A young newly wed girl was telling her friend how she had been teaching her husband to have better manners.
Suddenly she was interrupted by him rushing into the room and shouting,
"Come on, love, how about a quickie?"
Shocked, the girl's friend remarked, "I thought you were teaching him better manners?"
"I am," she stressed. "A month ago, he wouldn't have asked."

* * *

What will you never hear a man say?
I think we're lost, I'll pull over there and ask for directions.

* * *

MEN AT THEIR WORST

Few men marry their first love, and fewer marry their last.

* * *

"Boys will be boys - and so will a lot of middle-aged men."
Kin Hubbard

* * *

"All men are born truthful, and die liars."
Vauvenargues

* * *

"The best years are the forties; after fifty a man begins to deteriorate, but in the forties he is at the maximum of his villainy."
Mencken

* * *

Why do women rub their eyes when they get out of bed in the morning?
Because they don't have balls to scratch.

* * *

What's a jerk's definition of confidence?
When his wife discovers him in bed with another woman and he just smiles, slaps her on the backside and says, "You're next".

A courting couple had been together for more than six months but no matter how hard he tried, his girlfriend would not succumb to his sexual advances. Then one afternoon, he discovered how to overcome the problem, when he found out she loved fine jewellery. As they passed a jewellery shop, he said:
"Darling, if you let me make love to you, I will buy you that beautiful diamond ring."
At first she refused but the sight of this beautiful ring and his persuasive talk finally broke down her defences and they went back to his flat for a rough and tumble on the bed.
The following day they passed the jewellers and she reminded him of their deal. So in he went and came out with a ring that cost only a fraction of the piece they had been looking at the day before.
She ran home to her mother in tears and recounted the dreadful trick he had played on her.
"Oh my darling," sympathised her mother, "there's one thing about men you must never forget. When they're hard they're soft; and when they're soft, they're hard."

* * *

What eight words are said by more men, whatever their age?
"If you really loved me, you'd do it."

* * *

What are a jerk's favourite words?
"Nothing's going to happen that you don't really want to happen"
OR
"Trust me, I'll pull out at the right time."

* * *

A man stormed into a solicitor's office demanding they help him with his divorce.

"On what grounds?" they asked.
"She's got dirty habits," he replied, "and that's all I'm saying."
The solicitor explained that they would have to have more details to make the divorce successful for him.
"Oh, all right then" relented the man. "The fact is that every time I go to have a pee in the sink, it's always full of dishes."

* * *

How many Englishmen does it take to change a lightbulb?
What do you mean, change a light bulb? It's perfect. We've had it for 200 years and it's worked just fine.

* * *

A husband and wife have been married for 40 years and throughout their time together, the husband has pestered her for oral sex. But the wife has always refused, believing he would not respect her any more. So on the eve of their 40th wedding anniversary, he asks her again.
"Doris, after all these years, you know I love and respect you more than anything in the world. Just once, please, just once, let's have oral sex."
So the wife gives in and minutes after they've finished, the phone rings. The husband turns to his wife and remarks, "Hey, go answer the phone, you cocksucker."

* * *

An unscrupulous farmer had the hots for one of the dairymaids, so he decided to show her how he felt. He took her across to the field where his prize bull was servicing one of the cows, hoping to get the girl aroused.
After a few minutes, he looked at her with a leer in his eye and said, "I'd like to be doing what that bull is doing"
"Well, don't mind me," she said, "it's your cow."

Why are husbands like old cars?
They're hard to get started, very smelly and most of the time, they don't work.

* * *

Why do men get such a lot of exercise on the beach?
They're continually sucking in their stomachs every time they see a bikini.

* * *

An angry woman confronted her husband as he let himself into the house at 7 o'clock in the morning, smelling of alcohol, clothes awry and lipstick all over his face.
She snarled, "You'd better have a very good reason for coming in here at this time of the morning, looking like you do and stinking of alcohol."
"Oh, I do," he replied. "I'd like some breakfast."

* * *

Why are men like cockroaches?
They hang around the kitchen and are very difficult to get rid of.

* * *

A newly married couple arrive at the hotel for their honeymoon night and retire to the bedroom. The husband takes off his trousers, throws them at his new wife and says:
"Here, put these trousers on."
She looks at him astonished. "I can't wear these, they wouldn't fit."
"That's right," he replies. "Let's get this marriage off to a good start by remembering who wears the trousers."
A moment later, the new bride takes off her knickers and throws them at her husband.

"Here, Pete, put these on."
"Don't be silly, you know I couldn't get into those," he says.
"Dead right, you couldn't," she replies confidently, "and you never will get into them again if you don't change that ridiculous attitude."

* * *

Two women were serving on a market stall when a man rode up on a horse. He jumped down, tethered the horse to a railing, lifted the horse's tail and gave it a whacking big kiss on the arse.
Shocked, one of the women asked him why he had done such an awful thing.
"Dear ladies," he replied, "I've got chapped lips."
"Oh, is that some sort of cure for them?" they asked.
"Oh, no, but it stops me from licking them," he said.

* * *

Two women meet up in the street, not having seen each other for many years.
"So, Mary, did you ever get married?"
"Oh, yes," replied Mary, "I married an estate agent and an honest man too."
"Well, forgive me for asking, but isn't that bigamy?"

* * *

"Hello Jack, how's your wife?"
"I think she's dead."
"What do you mean, you think she's dead?"
"Well, the sex is still the same but the dishes are stacking up in the sink."

* * *

A couple stop at a motorway services for lunch. Once they're back on the road and 20 minutes have passed, the wife realises she has left her new leather gloves on the cafe table. She insists they go and get them and all the way back, the husband moans constantly about her stupidity.
"Bloody woman, just what you'd expect," he murmurs to himself all the time.
When they eventually arrive back at the services, she opens the door to get out and he leans over and says, "While you're there, you might as well pick up my glasses."

* * *

Two women talking on the top deck of a bus.
"I'll tell you one thing, May," said Pat. "Until I got married, I didn't think much of religion."
"Oh? What changed your mind?"
"I now believe in hell."

* * *

"All husbands are alike, but they have different faces so you can tell them apart."
Anon

* * *

The rugby stadium is crammed full of people waiting for the grand final. All the seats are taken except one towards the front of the stand. The newcomer makes his way towards the seat and says to the man next to it,
"Excuse me, is this seat free?"
"It is today," replies the man, "this is my wife's seat but she died a few days ago."
"Oh, I'm so very sorry," replies the newcomer. "Maybe you should have brought a friend along to keep you company."

"I would have done," answered the man, "but they're all at her funeral."

* * *

What's the difference between the Loch Ness monster and a good man?
The Loch Ness monster has, on the odd occasion, been seen.

* * *

Do you know what it means to come home to a loving husband who's got dinner on the table and a bottle of wine on ice?
Yes, it means you're in the wrong house.

* * *

"I used to take my wife all over the place," said the jerk, "but it doesn't work, she always finds her way home."

* * *

"Hey, Doreen!" shouted the woman from across the street, "do you like men who are bald on top but as hairy as gorillas everywhere else?"
"No!" shouted back Doreen.
"Well, do you like men who belch and fart constantly after every meal?" demanded the woman.
"Of course not," replied Doreen. "Why do you ask?"
"Oh, I just wondered why you were messing around with my husband."

* * *

Who's kidding who?
A woman had a very rich lover who was always lavishing expensive gifts on her. The other day he gave her a fur coat, which left her with the problem of how to explain away the gift to her husband. On the

way home, she came up with a great idea. She pawned the coat.
"Hello darling," she said, arriving home. " You'll never guess what happened today. As I was walking through the park, I bumped into a woman in great distress because she'd lost her winning lottery ticket. Somehow it had fallen out of her handbag. So we re-traced her steps and believe it or not, found the ticket caught in a bush. She was so grateful for my help, she gave me a pawn ticket which she said would be worth my while picking up. So darling, I wonder if you would collect the item, whatever it is, tomorrow when you're in town."
The next day, the husband returned home and presented his wife with a camera. The fur coat was now on the back of his secretary, who was delighted at her good fortune.

* * *

After a good romp in bed, the phone rang and the woman got out to answer it. A minute later she returned.
"Who was that?" asked the man.
"My husband."
"What! I'd better get going before he comes home."
"No hurry," she replied. "He said he was going to be late because he's playing darts with you."

* * *

Two men were sipping pints together in the pub. One was looking very miserable.
"Hey, Jack, what's wrong?" asked his mate.
"It's the wife," he replied. "Ever since she's started to go to the gym, she's cut sex down to once a week."
His mate retorted, "Well, think yourself lucky; she's cut me out altogether."

* * *

Three international countries were asked to carry out research into why a male penis has a head on it.
Italy spent the equivalent of half a million pounds and concluded that it was to give the woman more pleasure. America spent the equivalent of one million pounds and decided it was to give the man more pleasure. Australia spent just £100 and announced the head was there to keep your hand from sliding off.

* * *

Shaun went along to the priest for confession. He told the priest he'd slept with three different women in just seven days.
"What shall I do, Father?"
"Well, my son, when you leave here, go past the greengrocer's, buy a lemon and suck on it."
"Will my sins be forgiven then?" he asked in surprise.
"No," replied the priest, "but it'll take that damned silly grin off your face."

* * *

Men are often very stupid, always trying to be more macho than their fellow man.
One Friday, after drinking all afternoon, two men got into a very heated argument and to prove their manliness, they carried out more and more daring escapades. It started with smashing bricks with their bare hands, to dodging cars on the motorway, to wrestling with the wild dogs. Eventually feelings were running so high, one man picked up an electric saw and cut off his finger.
"Beat that!" he sneered, dripping with blood.
In a blind fury, the other picked up the saw, swung it above him and cut off his head.
"Ah, well," said the onlookers. "At school he was known as pansy Pete, he used to dress in his sister's clothes. At least he died like a man."

A man went to a reunion dinner and the hour was so late when it finished that one of the other guests invited him to stay over at his house.
The following day, he arrived home and was grilled by his jealous wife.
"What happened to you last night? Who were you with? Tell me."
Now the husband was in no mood for a cross examination, so he simply said:
"I stopped over with a friend and that's all you need to know."
Dissatisfied with this answer, she wrote to all the men at the reunion asking if her husband had stayed with them on the night of the dinner.
A day later she received all 20 replies saying "YES".

* * *

What's the similarity between birthdays and toilets?
Men always miss them.

* * *

What's a man's idea of safe sex?
Masturbation.

* * *

How many men does it take to change a toilet roll?
Who knows? It's never happened.

* * *

One day the local bully of a small town decided it was time to take a walk round his patch and flex a few muscles. Half way up the High Street, he came across a group of boys from the local college.
"Hey, you lot," he snarled, "who runs this place?"

"You do, Ted, you do," they quickly answered.

The bully moved on and bumped into a couple of local businessmen. "Watch it!" he yelled.

"Sorry, sorry, Ted," mumbled the men, shuffling away. "It was just an accident."

Time and time again, he bullied the local people. Then just as he was about to go into the pub for a pint, he came across a big gorilla of a bloke leaning against the lamp post.

"Hey, you," he said, swaggering over to him. "Ain't seen you round here before. Ted's my name and this is my patch. You know what that means, don't you?" he hissed.

All of a sudden, the big man picked Ted up by the scruff of the neck, knocked him against the wall and kicked him on the ground.

"OK, OK," gasped Ted, "no need to get so bloody angry just because you don't know the fucking answer."

MEN AT TRAVEL

A 'right Herbert' lorry driver picked up a female hitchhiker on the way to Manchester. Half way there, he put his hand on her knee and she said suggestively:
"You can go further if you like."
So he went as far as Carlisle.

* * *

A priest is travelling on a train when a man opposite engages him in conversation.
"Excuse me, I couldn't help but notice you've got your shirt on back to front."
"Oh, no," replies the priest, "I wear it like that because I'm a Father."
The man ponders this for a moment and then says, "But I'm a father too and I don't wear my shirt backwards."
The priest smiles, "Ah, yes, but I'm a Father of thousands."
"Well, in that case," retorts the man, "maybe you'd be better off wearing your underpants backwards."

* * *

The driver of the high speed train failed to switch off the intercom after welcoming passengers aboard the 6.15 to Paddington, so they all heard his next few words.
"As soon as I've filled these reports out, Steve, I'm going to take that new catering lass into the back room and give her a right good rogering."
Of course the woman involved was embarrassed and very angry when

she heard this and she raced up the train to confront the driver. However, on the way she tripped and fell over a suitcase that was sticking out into the aisle and ended up at the feet of an old woman.
"It's all right, dear," smiled the old woman, "no need to hurry; he says he's got to fill out some reports first."

* * *

A woman got onto a crowded train and asked a man sitting down whether she could have his seat because she was pregnant. He got up immediately and let her sit down, but after a couple of minutes he said, "Excuse me, but I must say, you don't look pregnant. How long has it been?"
The woman looked at her watch and replied, "About 35 minutes but it don't half make you tired."

* * *

The couple arrived at the airport with so much luggage it looked as if they were going away for two months rather than two weeks. As he viewed the cases, most of which were his wife's, he murmured, "I wish we'd brought the sideboard."
"All right, all right," she said sarcastically, "there's no need for that."
"No, I mean it," he said. "I left the tickets on it."

* * *

Two devout churchgoers are driving through a forest when all of a sudden a vampire bat lands on the bonnet of the car.
"Look at that, Harold," said Tom in alarm. "We must do something immediately. Quick, show it your cross."
"OK," said Harold. He wound down the window and bellowed, "Now look here, you damned bat, get off my bloody bonnet."

* * *

A long-time married couple boarded the train and found two spare seats in the front carriage. After a moment or two, the husband asked his wife, “Are you comfortable?”
“Yes, dear,” she replied.
“And is the seat soft enough?”
“Yes, thank you.”
“And it doesn’t move around?”
“Oh, no, dear.”
“Well, then, up you get and change places with me.”

* * *

A young businessman was returning home when his car broke down and he sought shelter in a nearby house. The following day he arrived back at work looking bleary-eyed and constantly yawning.
“What happened to you, then?” asked his mates.
The man explained about his car and the overnight stay at the nearby house.
“A young woman answered the door. She said she lived there alone and I was welcome to stop the night.”
“Oooh, oooh,” jeered his friends, “no wonder you look tired. A little bit of screwing went on, eh?”
“A lot,” replied the man. “When it was time for bed, she said the lock on her bedroom door was broken, so I spent half the night trying to mend it.”

* * *

Three men found themselves sharing a railway carriage - two friends and a stranger. After a few minutes one of the friends started scratching his arm and this scratching got progressively more frequent as time went on. Eventually they arrived at a station where the scratching man got off so it just left the other two in the carriage.
“My goodness,” said the stranger with some relief, “your friend seems to suffer badly.”

"Yes," agreed the other, "he's got terrible piles."
"No, no, I meant all the scratching on his arm."
"Yes, that's piles. You see he works for the government and he doesn't know his arse from his elbow."

* * *

A couple and their small son went on holiday and ended up on a nudist beach. While the wife lay down to sunbathe, the son walked off down the beach with his dad, but returned some time later to tell his mum that lots of the women had much bigger balloons than she had. Mum retorted quickly, "The bigger they are, the more stupid the woman."
Ten minutes later the little boy returned again.
"Mummy, mummy, I've seen lots of men with bigger willies than daddy's."
Again mum replied, "That's because the bigger they are, the more stupid they are."
So the afternoon passed peacefully until it was almost time to go, when suddenly the little boy raced back to his mother in panic.
"Oh, mum," he cried "what shall we do? I've just seen daddy talking to the most stupid lady on the beach, and the more he talks to her, the more stupid he gets."

* * *

A mother and her 19-year-old daughter were travelling in a railway carriage opposite a man who had both arms in plaster. Suddenly they heard the ticket collector coming up the passageway.
The man leaned forward and said, "Excuse me, ladies, I wonder if one of you will get my ticket out of my trouser pocket for me?"
"Go on, Julie," urged her mum, "help the man."
So Julie put her hand in his pocket but was so embarrassed, she dropped the ticket on the floor and it took some time to retrieve it from under the seat.

Later when the man had got off, mum turned to her daughter and said, "Julie, talk about making a drama out of a crisis! The poor man just needed some help."
"Oh, mother," replied the daughter, "I did feel such a big soft thing."

* * *

A man is driving through the wilds of Wales when he sees a huge gorilla of a man standing at the side of the road. Next to him is a beautiful young girl. They beckon for the man to stop, but as he does so, the car door is pulled open and he's dragged out onto the road.
"Right, you!" shouts the wild man. "I want you to masturbate."
In fear of his life, the driver does as he's told, but as soon as it's over, the wild man makes him do it again. This goes on for over an hour until the poor driver is left a broken wreck on the roadside.
"Again!" roars the wild man.
"I can't!" he gasps. "I don't care what you do to me now."
"OK," says the wild man, "now you can give my daughter a lift to Cardiff."

* * *

An old man was having trouble with his ears on his first air flight, so the stewardess brought him some chewing gum.
When they arrived at their destination, the stewardess asked him if he was all right.
"Fine thanks, but how do I get it out of my ears?"

* * *

The woman was wearing a very tight skirt, so when she tried to climb the stairs of the bus, she found she couldn't lift her leg. She reached behind her and unzipped her zip, but it didn't seem to make any difference. Again she reached behind her and unzipped it

further, when suddenly a man lifted her up and put her on the top step.

"How dare you!" she exclaimed.

"Well, miss, by the time you unzipped my fly for the second time, I thought we were good friends."

*** * ***

MEN AT WORK

After a month of daring armed robberies, the police finally catch the man responsible and take him down to the station for interrogation.
"So, just how much did you steal over this past month?" asks the officer.
"£200,000," he replies.
Over the next few days, the police carry out a thorough search of his house and discover nearly £300,000 in cash. When they inform him of their find and accuse him of still hiding the truth, he replies:
"Yes, but you've got to remember, I'm a builder by trade. It was only an estimate."

* * *

A driver is pulled over for speeding and asked to take the breathalyser. As he is doing this, the policeman notices a set of sharp knives on the back seat of the car and thinks it highly suspicious.
"Excuse me sir," he says. "Why have you got a set of knives in the back of your car?"
"It's my job, officer," replies the man. "I'm a juggler."
"Well, in that case, just to ensure everything is as you say, will you please get them out and show me your act?"
So the next moment, the driver is juggling the knives at the side of the road, when another car passes by.
"Hell fire!" exclaims the second motorist. "Did you see that, Mabel? I'm so glad I packed in drinking; look at the tests they make you do now."

* * *

The milkman walks up the path of number 47 to see a note pinned to the door requesting 50 gallons of milk.
He knocks on the door and it is opened by a beautiful woman wearing only a towel.
"Excuse me, miss, is it true you want 50 gallons of milk?"
"That's right. I've been reading in a magazine that if you bathe in milk, your skin will make you look ten years younger."
"Really!" replied the milkman. "And do you want that pasteurised?"
"No, just up to my tits will do."

* * *

A businessman attended a special company dinner and was asked by the chairman to step in at the last moment to say a few words, because the original speaker had fallen ill.
The man thought quickly and decided to talk about sex. It was a great success.
Later, when he arrived home, his wife asked him how the dinner went and he told her he had to get up and speak.
"Oh? And what did you talk about?"
Knowing how prudish his wife could be, he replied, "Golf."
The following week, his wife met Geraldine, the chairman's wife.
"Janet, how nice to see you," said Geraldine. "May I just say again how much we all enjoyed the speech your husband gave last week."
"Thank you. I am really quite surprised. He's only done it once and ended up losing his balls."

* * *

The puny policeman stopped a man in the street and said, "Excuse me sir, I'll have to ask you to come down to the police station."
"But why? I haven't done anything wrong."
"I know, but it's really dark and foggy tonight and I'm afraid to go there on my own."

A man takes his sick dog to the vet's and after ten minutes of examining the poor animal, the vet returns to the waiting room to speak to its owner.
"Excuse me, sir, but could you please say 'aah' for me?"
"Yes, but why should I say 'aah'?"
"Because your dog's just died," he replied.

* * *

A rich millionaire woke up one morning to find 'Martin's a wanker' written in the snow in urine. He immediately called his private secretary.
"Hodges, test this straight away. I want to know who this is," he raged.
Later that day, Hodges returned, somewhat embarrassed.
"Well?" demanded the millionaire. "Come on man, spit it out, who's the culprit?"
"Well, sir," he stammered. "The urine is the gardener's, but the handwriting is your wife's."

* * *

"That was a wonderful weekend we spent in Paris," said the boss to his secretary. "Will you ever be able to forget it?"
"Depends how much it's worth," she replied.

* * *

Two brothers had been working in the sawmill for just a week when one shouted out in pain.
"Aagh! Mat, Mat, I've cut my finger off."
Mat came rushing over. "Bloody hell," he said, "how did you do that?"
"I just touched this wheel here like this and... shit, there goes another one."

* * *

The boss walked into the office smiling broadly and told his workers a new joke he had recently heard. As he gave them the punchline, they all collapsed in peals of laughter except one woman by the filing cabinet.
Immediately the boss demanded what was wrong.
"Have you got no sense of humour?" he asked.
"Oh, yes," she replied, "a good one, but I don't need to laugh; I'm leaving at the end of the week."

* * *

Why did the man get the sack from the M&M factory?
He kept throwing away all the W's.

* * *

A group of ramblers were walking across a field when they caught sight of the farmer driving his tractor without any trousers on.
They called out to him.
"Good morning, farmer, we couldn't help but notice that you aren't wearing any trousers. Do you mind if we ask why that is?"
"Not at all," said the farmer, grinning mischievously.
"It's the damnedest thing. Last week I was out ploughing all day and the weather was so hot, I didn't bother wearing a shirt. By the time I got home, my poor neck was as stiff as a poker. So this is my wife's idea."

* * *

A man goes for a job as a lumberjack and is told by the boss that he has to prove himself by cutting down 100 trees in a day.
So the next day, the man takes the chain saw into the woods and happily works there until dusk, but when the trees are counted up, there are only 98. The boss tells him to try again the following day but he only fells 99.

"I don't know what you're doing wrong. Come out with me tomorrow," says the boss, "and you can see how I do it."
So the next morning they both go out to the woods. The boss takes the chain saw and starts up the engine.
"Hey, what's that noise?" asks the man.

* * *

Driving well above the speed limit, the woman suddenly heard the familiar sound of the police siren as she was beckoned onto the hard shoulder. She thought quickly and decided to try and lighten the situation by cracking a joke. As the policeman walked up to her car, she rolled down the window and said, smiling, "I know, officer, you've come over to ask me to the policemen's ball!"
The policeman replied, "Cops don't have balls."
There was an awful moment of silence, then without saying another word, the officer turned round and walked back to his car.

* * *

Two male croupiers were standing idle at the craps table when a beautiful woman approached. She wanted to bet £10,000 on a single roll of the dice.
"I hope you won't mind," she said smiling, "but I always feel much luckier if I bet when I'm not wearing any clothes." And with that, she took off her coat to reveal her naked body underneath. Then she threw the dice.
"I won, I won!" she cried ecstatically, kissing each of the croupiers on the lips. Then she picked up her winnings and walked away.
After a moment of stunned silence, the croupiers looked at each other and one asked, "What did she roll anyway?"
"I don't know, I don't know," replied the other. "I thought you were watching."

* * *

An old farmer, much set in his ways, was advised that there was an acute shortage of bulls and he ought to think about artificial insemination. Now the poor old farmer had no idea what this meant but rang up the vet to arrange a time. When the vet realised this was all new to the man, he gave him strict instructions.
"Make sure the cowshed is as clean as it can possibly be, wash down the cow thoroughly and provide a bucket of hot water and some towels."
So the farmer did as was told and the next day the vet arrived at the appointed hour.
"I've done as you asked," said the farmer proudly, "and I've even put a hook behind the door."
"A hook?" queried the vet. "What for?"
"Well, to hang your trousers up. I'm sure you don't want them left on the floor."

* * *

A man went to apply for a driving licence and was highly embarrassed when the official asked him for his full name. After some hesitation, he replied quietly:
"Peter bloody hell that hurts Jones."
The official looked up in surprise and asked him how he got such a name. The man explained: "As the vicar was christening me, the top of the font slid off the side and landed on his foot."

* * *

The butcher's wares were laid out in front of the shop for customers to pick the piece of meat they preferred and bring it inside for payment.
It had been a very busy morning. Customers had been in and out non-stop, but one woman in particular caught the butcher's eye. She had walked up and down the display for more than five minutes, picking up each piece of meat in turn, poking it, picking it up again, putting it down...

Eventually the butcher came out of his shop and said to her. "Come on, Madam, make your mind up; it's not like your hubby you know; it won't grow larger the longer you play with it."

* * *

There was a man who lived for his work; it was the most important thing in his life. One lunchtime, he met up for drinks with an old friend and soon the talk got round to business.
"So how's work?" asked the friend.
"Very good," enthused the man. "I've taken on a new finance manager and he's absolutely brilliant. The only problem is that he's made two of the office girls pregnant, split up another family and seduced my own daughter!"
"Bloody hell!" exclaimed the friend. "What are you going to do about it?"
"Don't worry," laughed the man. "I'm watching him very carefully and if I find him fiddling the company in any way, he'll be sacked on the spot."

* * *

Why do men get paid twice as much as women for doing the same job?
Women do it right the first time.

* * *

What would men do if they had breasts?
Never go to work but stay at home all day playing with them.

* * *